D1053603

Mary Jemison: Seneca Captive

by the same author

SKY PIONEERS: The Story of Wilbur and Orville Wright

Jeanne LeMonnier Gardner

Mary Jemison
SENECA CAPTIVE

ILLUSTRATED BY ROBERT PARKER

HARCOURT, BRACE & WORLD, INC., NEW YORK

For Richard,
with love

Cabin that Mary Jemison helped to build
for her daughter at Gardeau

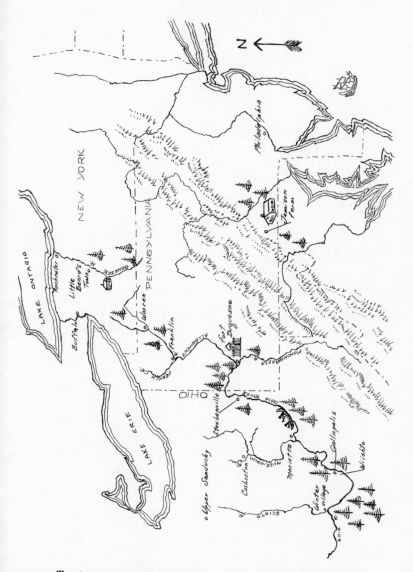

Territory through which Mary Jemison journeyed

Mary Jemison : Seneca Captive

One

Mary Jemison felt the new warmth of an April sun as she approached the edge of the clearing. At the far end of the field, furrowed into black ribbons of freshly turned soil, her father and her older brothers, John and Thomas, Jr., labored behind a team of horses pulling a heavy wooden plow.

Mary cupped her hands around her mouth to make her voice carry. "Pa! Pa!" she called loudly. "Supper's almost ready. Ma wants you and the boys back at the house now."

Thomas Jemison raised an arm in greeting at his daughter's message, and Mary sat down on a stump to wait for him. She watched the slow procession of men and horses travel the length of a furrow. One of the horses limped, and the men walked with wearisome steps. The full strength of two of them was needed to hold the plow steady as it lifted the heavy black sod. Pa said the soil was rich—as rich as he ever hoped to farm.

Mary looked beyond the field to the sloping hills

that rose and fell throughout the Pennsylvania countryside. Pa loved the land! That was sure! He and Mary's mother had traveled a long way to find it. In 1743 they had crossed the ocean from Ireland to search out a homestead in the English Colonies of the New World. Mary had been born during the perilous sea voyage on board the tiny sailing vessel *Mary William*, as it tossed between the pounding waves of the Atlantic Ocean. Pa had often teased Mary about arriving in the world on stormy seas. "A stormy life you'll be leading," he'd say to her with a merry gleam in his eyes and a teasing tone in his voice.

The Jemison farm at the head of Marsh Creek in what is now Adams County, Pennsylvania, had once been part of hunting grounds belonging to Indians of the Delaware and Shawnee tribes. Some years earlier, as white settlers had begun to encroach upon the land, the Indians had withdrawn to seek freer hunting lands in the Ohio Valley west of the great Appalachian Mountain barrier. Though the Jemisons had farmed the land for more than a dozen years, the area was still, in the year 1758, regarded as frontier country. The scattered settlers there lived lonely pioneer lives, attending to their own needs for food and clothing, shelter and survival. Only the fur traders dared to venture beyond the foothills into the mountains. For the past few years, however, even the boldest of the traders hesitated to risk death bartering for the skins of beaver and bear. There was no telling any more whether an Indian would greet a trader with welcome or with the scalping knife.

These were years of bitter conflict between England and France, which would be known in American history as the French and Indian Wars. The struggle between the rival European nations for possession of lands in the New World had been going on for over half a century. Before that, the same lands had been fought for, over and over, by Indian tribes and possessed by the conquerors among them. Now the English wanted the Indians to help them drive the French from the land, and the French tried to bribe the Indians to help them wipe out the English.

Many of the tribes that had been friendly to the settlers in the English colonies now turned against them and allied themselves with the French. War parties of French soldiers and Indian warriors terrorized settlers in the Pennsylvania valley lands, but so far, the raiding parties had not come near the Jemison farm.

When the Jemison men reached the spot where Mary waited for them, Pa reached out his hand to stroke his daughter's long flaxen hair. It was a gesture of habit. Often he had likened her hair to the ripened grain that glistened in a midday sun.

Mary had to double-step to keep up with her father's long strides on their way back to the house. She was small for a girl of fifteen—only four and a half feet tall. She sensed by the set of her father's jaw and by the glint of his blue Irish eyes that he was pleased with the day's work. Since sunup he and his tall sons had been readying the fields to receive the flax seeds that would later grow to bear pale blue blossoms.

Mary wished she had been allowed to help with the planting instead of working inside at the sewing and mending with her mother and her older sister, Betsey. She liked the planting and hoeing of flax much more than she did the tedious hours of spinning it into thread and weaving the thread into coarse linen cloth. She already looked forward to helping Pa with the weeding in a few weeks' time. In the springtime Pa needed help from the whole family to keep weeds from choking out the tender shoots of the young seedlings. How she and Betsey had giggled last spring at the feel of the newly loosened soil, soft and squiggly beneath their toes, as they had trod carefully through the rows pulling out weeds.

As if he had sensed her thoughts, Thomas Jemison slowed his steps and spoke solemnly. Mary wasn't sure if he was speaking so much to her as he was to himself.

"It's a good life, child," he said with a wistful glance backward at the tilled acres. "The soil is rich. The land is fair to look at. A man's free to live as he chooses here and to raise his family as he sees fit."

"That's why we came, isn't it, Pa?" Mary asked.

"Yes, child," he said, and for a moment a faraway look came into his eyes. Then, from a distance a voice called. "That's your mother, Mary. Run on ahead and tell her we'll be in as soon as we put the animals in the barn. I must examine the mare's hoof."

Mary lingered a moment. "Ma's awful skittery these days, Pa," she said. "There's more talk of Indians . . ."

"Yes, I know," the tall man interrupted her. "Your mother worries too much. We've not been troubled here by any Indians, and I don't figure we're going to be. Now go see what you can do to help with supper. The boys and I will be along in a minute."

Mary's hair bounced on her shoulders as she skipped toward her mother at the cabin door. "Pa's coming in a minute," she said with a bright smile. "He's plowed more than half the flax field, Ma. Do you think if I ask him he'll let me help with the rest of the planting?"

"You'd better wait till after supper before you ask him," her mother cautioned. "The seeds are scarce, and he's mighty fussy about how they're sown. Come along now and help Betsey and me put supper on the table."

Mary sniffed hungrily at the simmering contents of the iron kettle that hung over the fire on the hearth. Venison stew! The fresh deer meat had provided a rare treat to the Jemisons for the past week or so—ever since the day Pa had spotted the deer near the far edge of the clearing and shot it with his musket. It was the

15

first red meat they'd had in a long time. Pa did not often hunt the wooded hills beyond sight of the cabin nowadays.

"Oh, Ma! You made corn bread, too!" Mary exclaimed.

"Mary Jemison! I'll not be having you call me Ma!" Mrs. Jemison said with a mixture of annoyance and humor in her voice.

"I keep forgetting. I'm sorry, Mother," Mary said.

"Call Matthew and Robert to the table, please," Mrs. Jemison said, "while Betsey and I dish up the stew."

Eight Jemisons with bowed heads sat at the long rough plank table while Mr. Jemison said the blessing: "We thank Thee, Lord, for this meal of which we are about to partake and for the bountiful land which yielded it through Thy blessings, Amen."

For a few moments, while the family ate the hearty stew from wooden trenchers and sopped up its gravy with corn bread, the only sounds in the room were those of the fire crackling in the hearth and the muffled din of spoons scraping the wood of the bowls.

When the meal was finished, Mr. Jemison cleared his throat and spoke to the two small boys who were the youngest of his six children.

"Matthew, Robert," he said, looking in turn at each of them, "I want you to help Betsey redd up the chicken yard as soon as supper's cleared away."

Mrs. Jemison interrupted. "And mind you, don't go wandering off!"

"Mary," he continued, pausing only long enough for Mary to look up and meet his gaze, "you're to go over to neighbor Tilghmans' and ask him for the loan of his horse. Tell him I'll return it late tomorrow afternoon."

"*No*, Thomas!" cried Mrs. Jemison. "It will be dark before she can get back! I don't want her going alone. It's not safe!"

"Now, Jane," said Mr. Jemison, "you get upset over nothing. It's only a mile or so, and she can be there and back before nightfall if she doesn't dawdle."

"Can't one of the older boys go?" Mrs. Jemison persisted.

"I need them here," her husband said firmly. "But if it would make you rest easier, Mary can spend the night at the Tilghmans' and bring the horse back first thing in the morning."

The lines of weary resignation around her faded blue eyes made Jane Erwin Jemison look old. She was a small red-haired woman whose skin, once pink and delicate, was now creased with the wrinkles of a woman twice her age. She had borne the hardships of pioneer life without complaint until the Indian troubles had grown worse. Then she had begun to urge her husband to leave the farm and move back east. Though she knew her arguments were useless, she was unable to hide from the family her fears for their safety.

"Sometimes I wish we had never left Ireland," she said in a small, pitiful voice. "We lived among *civilized* people there. To think we came all this way to risk our necks—and our scalps—among savage Indians . . ." She broke off with a shudder.

"You are forgetting, my dear," her husband chided gently, "that we lived with cruelties in the Old Country, too."

Mrs. Jemison was silent as her thoughts dwelt on the truth of Thomas's remark.

"Were there Indians in Ireland, too?" young Matthew asked. The other children sat quietly, hoping Pa would tell them more about the island country across the ocean where he and their mother had grown up and where Betsey and John and Thomas had been born.

"No, son," Mr. Jemison replied. "There were no Indians. But there were soldiers sent by the English king to rob the Irish people of their farms and to loot their homes. Then, when the people could not pay taxes and fines, they were whipped and thrown into jails."

"Did you have to pay taxes and fines, too?" Robert asked.

"Aye, and more than we could afford," said Mr. Jemison. "But we were better off than most. There were thousands of Irish families driven from their homes," he recounted. "They were left without food, without money, and without work. They lived in such dreadful poverty that many of the finest citizens were forced to become beggars in the city streets."

"Why didn't the people fight back, Pa?" asked Matthew.

"They tried, son," he said, "but the English armies were organized and powerful. The people of Ireland were not able to defend themselves against them. Their farmlands were confiscated, and they found themselves tenant-farmers on their own land, paying tributes to greedy English noblemen. They had barely enough left to keep their own families from starving."

Mr. Jemison sounded angry now. "Anyone with ambition," he went on, "left Ireland—just as we did. And now that we have good land and a comfortable home, I'm not willing to give it up!"

Mary saw that as her father spoke these last words, his hands clenched into tight fists. While she studied the intense scowl that creased his brow, his blue eyes met hers of the same color, and his expression softened. A broad smile spread across his angular face.

"Your ma and I don't always agree about settling this far west, child," he said gently, "but we did right by leaving Ireland." He looked tenderly at his wife. "Didn't we, Janie? We stand together on that, don't we?"

"Tom Jemison!" his wife said to him in pretended

scorn but with a lilt in her voice. "You always did have a way with you." She smiled at her husband, and the tension in her face eased.

"You be on your way to the Tilghmans' now," Mr. Jemison said gently to Mary. "Come back with the horse first thing in the morning, and be sure to tell Mr. Tilghman that I'm mighty obliged to him."

"All right, Pa," Mary said.

Mrs. Jemison handed Mary a woolen shawl that hung from a peg inside the door. "You'd better take this," she said. "The sun will be down soon, and you'll need it to keep off the chill."

"Thank you, Ma." Mary kissed her mother and went on talking as she started out the door of the house. "Don't worry any. I won't be scared, and it will be fun staying at the Tilghmans'. I'll be home soon after sun-up."

"Promise me you'll not loiter on the way," Mrs. Jemison said anxiously.

With her long yellow hair flying behind her as she skipped through the yard, Mary turned and called back, "I promise, Ma."

Two

Mary followed the path that led eastward along the upper banks of Marsh Creek toward the Tilghman homestead. Behind her the sun dropped lower and lower into the mountain ridges. Shadows lengthened on the moving waters of the creek, grown wide with spring thaws and April rains.

The path had been one of the branches of an old Indian trail that threaded across the landscape. Mary knew it by heart. She had walked it at least a hundred times going back and forth to the Tilghmans' on errands for Ma.

It was good to be away from the house! A smile curled the corners of her mouth as she thought of her mother's remark to Pa at the supper table.

"I wish Ma laughed more often," Mary thought. "She looks pretty when she laughs. Younger, too. If only she weren't so worried and scared all the time."

The path narrowed as it entered the thicket of mountain laurel that grew at the edge of the woodland. Tall dark hemlocks shut out the twilight sky. Mary walked a little faster beneath their drooping branches. Underfoot, the moist brown earth was soft with a covering of tree needles shed during the winter by the great evergreens.

The sound of the rushing creek waters grew fainter as Mary moved through the darkening stretches of the woods. New sounds caught her attention. She paused to peer uneasily over her shoulder. Were the little noises behind her only the familiar rustlings of the squirrels, or had the woods become unfriendly?

Her mother's fears darted through her mind. "It's not safe," she had said. Mary stared straight into the thicket ahead and quickened her steps. She recalled the grownups' talk about what had happened to people captured by Indians. Entire families were killed, often brutally—sometimes by being tied to a stake and burned alive. Homes and barns were set ablaze and cattle ruthlessly slaughtered. Sometimes young children were spared the scalping knife only to be carried off as captives.

Mary shuddered. She tried to blot out the scenes her mind pictured. They would not go away. Now, as dusk settled like an umbrella over the forest, every shadow became a menacing enemy, every rustle of the branches a new terror. Never before had the woods seemed so eerie or the path so long and winding. Fearfully Mary scooped up the skirts of her dress and began to run.

Her heart pounded as she raced—half stumbling—toward the clearing that lay at the other end of the forest, where the trail returned to the banks of the creek near the Tilghmans' home.

In terror she ran until she emerged safely into the clearing. And still she ran, not noticing the chickens in the field nor the sheets drying on the clothesline. She glanced back. At that moment she felt herself caught by smothering folds. She had run headlong into a sheet.

Helplessly she flailed at the firm cloth. It wound about her, holding her tightly. Terror stricken, she finally dropped to the ground in a faint.

"Mary. Mary Jemison. Wake up, child."

Mary snuggled deeper into the quilts piled on top of her.

"You've had a scare, child." Mrs. Tilghman's voice spoke softly. "And you've given *us* a scare. Everything is all right, Mary. Wake up now."

Mary stirred in the warm bed. She blinked her eyes feebly as her senses slowly returned to her. It was daylight.

"Oh, Mrs. Tilghman. I'm sorry. What happened to me? I was coming through the woods, and I started thinking about Indians . . . and I began to run . . . and. . . ." Her voice trailed off. "That's the last I can remember," she finished.

"Well, child," Mr. Tilghman spoke up, "you came streaking into our yard last evening like a bear chased by bees, and you ran smack into one of Mrs. Tilghman's bed linens hanging on a line. You fainted dead away, and our boy Patrick found you crumpled on the ground. He carried you in, and Mrs. Tilghman put you to bed. You had us all scared. We couldn't bring you around to your senses."

Mary blushed. She had just noticed the tall red-haired Patrick standing in the corner. "I can't imagine why I fainted," she said in a tone of embarrassment. "I've never done that before."

"I'd have been scared, too." Patrick's voice held none of the mockery Mary had anticipated. "You shouldn't have been out alone so late in the day. It was almost dark when you got here. No one goes through the woods any more without feeling skittery."

"What brought you out, Mary?" asked Mr. Tilghman. "Is everything all right at home?" There was a hint of anxiety in his voice.

"Everything's all right, Mr. Tilghman," Mary said. "Pa and Tom and John have begun the plowing, and one of Pa's horses has something wrong with its hoof. Pa sent me to borrow a horse from you. He said he'd be mighty obliged to you and that he'd bring it back later in the day."

"Well, in that case, he'll be wanting it right away," Mr. Tilghman replied. "Pat," he said, turning to his son, "come along and help me saddle the gelding."

"You get dressed now, Mary," Mr. Tilghman said, "and Mrs. Tilghman will have a bite of breakfast ready for you before you start for home."

Mary dressed hurriedly. She felt foolish for the panic that had caused her to faint in the Tilghmans' yard. She was glad that Patrick had not teased her. "Ma would understand, though," she thought, and it was comforting. "But I won't tell her," she decided aloud. "She's so worried all the time as it is. It wouldn't be right."

Half an hour later the Tilghman family stood in their yard waving good-by to Mary and calling out last-minute messages to be given to the Jemisons. Mary rode off feeling tall and alert on the horse.

The forest held none of the terrible foreboding that had engulfed her the evening before. Early morning sunlight sifted through tree branches, brightening the yellow-green needles that grew new at the tips of the hemlock sprays. Patches of olive-green moss were clumped on rocks, and from her position high atop the horse, she could see tender ferns uncurling their lacy fronds on the forest floor. Spring painted its portrait of newness everywhere.

As she came in sight of her home, Mary noticed the swollen buds of the apple and peach trees that grew in the orchard beyond the barn. Only a few days more in the sun and the clustered buds would burst open into an array of springtime blossoms. She inhaled deeply, hoping for a hint of the perfume that would soon fill the air.

Behind the large log barn she saw Tom, Jr., and John at work repairing a wooden rake. Then her eye traveled across the farmyard to the side of the house, where Pa was bent over a slender length of hickory wood, shaping it into a handle for the ax. He was talking to a man Mary had never seen before.

"Good day, Pa," Mary called across the yard.

"Ah, I'm glad you're back, child," her father said warmly. He put down his work and got up to help Mary dismount. "Your mother will be relieved to see you, too." He gave her head a gentle stroke. "Run on inside so she'll know you're back safe."

"Yes, Pa," Mary said. She paused. She was curious about the stranger.

"This is Mr. Buck, Mary. He's a new neighbor, and he's brought his sister-in-law and her young 'uns to stay with us for a while." Mr. Jemison completed the introduction: "William, this is my daughter, Mary."

"Howdy, Miss Jemison," Mr. Buck said.

"How do you do," Mary replied with politeness. She wondered why the visitors had come, and she lingered a moment longer hoping Pa or Mr. Buck might say something that would tell her more.

Mr. Jemison handed the reins of the horse to Mr. Buck and returned to his work shaving the ax helve.

"You might as well go for that bag of grain at your place now," he said to him.

"I reckon so," Mr. Buck replied, somewhat reluctantly. "I'll take my gun along." As if to satisfy the quizzical look on Mary's face, he added, "Just in case I come upon some game. I reckon Mrs. Jemison and my sister-in-law will welcome fresh meat to help feed so many mouths."

Looking up from his work, Mr. Jemison broke in before Mr. Buck could say more. "Don't keep your mother waiting any longer, Mary. She's been worried about you."

"All right, Pa." Mary started around the corner of the house toward the door as Mr. Buck was about to ride off on his errand.

Inside the house Mary was greeted with the cheerful confusion of breakfast preparations being carried on in the presence of guests. On the far side of the room, Matthew and Robert were absorbed in swapping boastful tales with a boy who looked to be about nine years old. A small dark-haired girl of about four sat cross-legged on the floor near them. She turned a curious wide-eyed gaze on Mary as she hung her shawl on the peg inside the door.

Across the room in front of the great fireplace with its chimney of stones chinked with dried mud, Mrs. Jemison stooped to turn a pan of muffins. A tall thin woman holding a young child in her arms was saying to her, "My, that smells good." And she added in a more solemn tone, "You have no idea how grateful I am for your hospitality to us."

"There's room enough, Mrs. Mann, and we're happy to be able to help you and your children," Mrs. Jemison answered as she straightened up from her crouched position at the hearth. She saw Mary then, and she closed her eyes slowly for a moment, breathing out a long, audible sigh of gratitude and relief. Mrs. Jemison's faded blue eyes told Mary more clearly than words the anxiety that her mother had endured throughout the night.

An instant later, musket shots outside the house shattered the morning air.

Three

Mary saw her mother's expression change from joy to terror. The color drained from her face. Mary was afraid that her mother was going to faint, and she reached out to support her. Then she eased her onto a footstool near the hearth before turning toward the door to investigate the cause of the gunshots. At the sight before her, she stiffened.

An Indian warrior filled the doorway. In his hand was a tomahawk, raised and ready to strike. Black war paint in zigzag designs made a grotesque mask of his face. His head was shaved except for a tuft of stiff black hair that grew from the top of his scalp. It was bound with a pouf of eagle feathers. His only clothing consisted of moccasins and a deerskin breechclout that hung like a small apron from a belt dotted with shell beads. The rest of his body was naked and streaked boldly with red, black, and yellow war paint. His bronzed skin shone like copper in the light of the morning sun filtering through the doorway. His eyes flashed as they scanned the room and its occupants. Then,

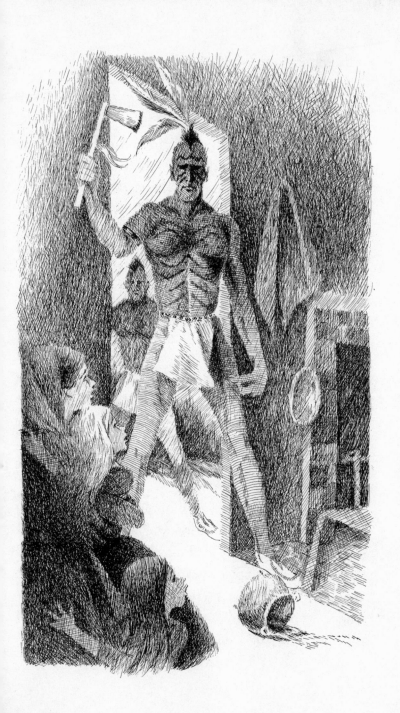

with a threatening flourish of his tomahawk, he strode arrogantly inside.

Five more warriors followed him. They were smeared with war paint also and carried cruel-looking knives and hatchets. A harsh, gutteral command from the leader sent them shuffling around the house, poking into bins and cupboards and rifling through the contents of drawers and cabinets.

Mary stood near the hearth beside her mother, frozen with fear. She had tried to scream, but no sound came from her throat.

The dark-haired little girl, who had stared at Mary a moment ago when she had arrived, ran to her mother's side and stood screaming while her small hands tore at the woman's skirts. Mary saw one of the Indians scowl menacingly at the little girl. Mrs. Mann saw the look, too, and pulled her child close to quiet her. The two Jemison boys and their new friend huddled together—their swaggering tales silenced now by the awesome reality of the adventure taking place before them.

Mary shut her eyes tight, hoping she would open them to find it was all a dream. The whimperings of the children and the shuffling of moccasined feet on the wooden floor, however, made dreaming impossible. What would happen to them? Where was Pa? And where were her older brothers? Mary pictured Pa stalking boldly into the house with John and Thomas to save them. Surely they would come soon! Then a horrible fear erased the vision. Suppose the gunshots outside had hurt Pa!

Mary counted. There were six Indians. Outside there were her father and the stranger he had introduced as Mr. Buck. Mr. Buck was going somewhere to get a bag of grain. Maybe he hadn't gone yet. And there were Tom and John. That would be four men against six Indians. The younger children didn't count. They weren't old enough or big enough to be of help. But *she* could help. So could Betsey and Ma and Mrs. Mann. And maybe Mr. Buck had ridden off just as the Indians arrived. Perhaps he was already on his way back, bringing help. Maybe. Just maybe.

In the buoyancy of hope, Mary stood as straight and tall as she could. And she prayed. She could tell that Ma was praying, too.

Just the same, she was scared. An Indian attack was the horror her mother had dreaded. This was what Ma and Pa had whispered about at night when the children were supposed to be asleep. And this was what they had argued about, too—Ma wanting to go back to Philadelphia where it was safe and Pa insisting that they were still safe here.

In her terror Mary clutched at her mother's shoulder. Mrs. Jemison placed her own hand on her daughter's in a gesture of comfort. There was strength in the gesture. Their eyes met, and Mary was surprised to see the look her mother gave her. It seemed to say, "Be strong. Don't be afraid." It made Mary feel better. She was able to control her trembling now, and she lifted her chin an inch higher to help hide her fear. She could even smell the breakfast muffins, though she was not hungry.

The Indians continued to poke around the house helping themselves to whatever they wanted. The leader, who stood guard over the helpless women and children, said something Mary couldn't understand. Then the other Indians began to hurry in their search for plunder. They dumped drawers onto the floor. They kicked over chairs that were in their way and gathered up whatever they could carry. Mostly it was food they took—meal, dried meat, bread.

One of them knocked over Ma's blue Delft pitcher. It shattered into pieces on the floor. Another kicked at the spinning wheel, knocking the bobbin off its spindle and sending it rolling across the floor—the coarse linen thread unwinding in a curling trail. One warrior slashed Ma's favorite patchwork quilt—the one done in the triple Irish Chain pattern.

Mary felt hot angry tears well up in her eyes. Even though she knew anger was useless, it came as a relief from the sick fear deep in the pit of her stomach. She looked across the room at her sister. Betsey was twisting the hem of her white apron until it had been wrung into a coil. She kept her head lowered, her eyes toward the floor.

A second command from the Indian leader sent three of the warriors stomping outside, their arms laden with foodstuffs they had looted. The leader went outside, too, leaving two Indian braves to stand guard inside the house. One of them took up his post just inside the door. The other, small and wiry with an ugly scar running from the corner of his left eye to beneath his chin, walked stealthily around the room with one hand poised above the handle of the knife in his belt. What had seemed a long and horrible interim was, in reality, only a few minutes' time.

Through the open door Mary could hear voices. Mingled with the gruntlike sounds of Indian words were other words spoken rapidly in a strange-sounding language. She listened intently, hoping to hear a word here and there that she could understand. Everyone in the room remained silent, listening. They sensed their fate was being decided by the exchange of unknown tongues outside.

The waiting lasted forever, Mary thought. It was only a moment later, however, when the leader poked his head inside and motioned to his comrades to bring the women and children outside.

Mary shuddered at what she saw. Crumpled on the ground was the body of Mr. Buck. He had been shot several times. Beside him lay the body of the horse she had borrowed for Pa from the Tilghmans and ridden home only a short while ago. Mary began trembling again as she huddled close to Ma and the children. Her eyes searched frantically for Pa. Then she saw him. He was alive. Thank God, Pa was alive! "Ma, do you see?" Mary whispered. "Pa's all right!" Mr. Jemison was slumped against the far corner of the house, his arms bound firmly to his sides with leather thongs. He stared vacantly at the scene before him as if in a trance, but he seemed to be unharmed.

Four white men were talking with the Indian leader. When Mary saw them, she thought for a moment that they had come to save them. Her new hope vanished quickly, however. The white men dressed in buckskins were soldiers—French soldiers who had come with the Indians as part of the raiding party.

The parley between the Frenchmen and the Indians grew louder. The soldiers waved their hands about as they talked. They appeared to be arguing in sharp disagreement over what to do with their prisoners. Then the babble of voices and the wild gesturing stopped abruptly. They had come to an agreement.

Four

From the moment the prisoners were herded away from the Jemison home, it was evident that the Indians and the four Frenchmen were in a great hurry. They had not even taken time to set fire to the house and barn. Instead, they hastened their captives toward the thick cover of the woods, pushing and poking them into a half run.

Mrs. Jemison took hold of young Matthew, helping him along at a pace his little legs could manage only with strenuous effort. Betsey helped Robert. Mrs. Mann carried her smallest child, and Mary helped by taking the arm of the little girl. The child had begun to bawl again, but Mary quieted her until her sobs subsided into a faint whimper. Mrs. Mann's boy, Will, was able to keep up by himself. Mr. Jemison staggered along as best he could, his eyes blinking in silent disbelief at what was happening. His arms were still bound to his sides, making his movements awkward and unbalanced.

The little girl holding Mary's hand tripped on a tree

root and fell. Mary helped her to her feet and kept a firmer hold on her as they hurried along. She looked over her shoulder time and again for a sign of her older brothers. The war party had led the captives in the opposite direction from the barn. Mary knew that John and Tom, Jr., had been working behind it a short while before, but now it was impossible to know if they lay dead and scalped or if they had escaped. Mary hoped and prayed that they were safe.

The prisoners struggled to maintain the grueling pace set by the war party. The trail was narrow and overgrown. In places there appeared to be no trail at all. Keeping up was especially hard for the smallest children. Whenever one of them lagged behind, he received a stinging lash against his legs from a whip carried by the Indian who brought up the rear.

Thirst began to bother the children. They begged for water, but their pleas were unheeded. Even when the trail ran alongside or across a small stream, they were not given time to drink. They were hungry, too, for they had had no breakfast that morning. The forced march continued relentlessly. No food. No water. No rest. All morning and all afternoon the weary party pushed through the forest at a running pace. Finally, when it grew too dark to see where they were going, they were halted and forced to lie upon the bare ground. They were given no food or water throughout the night's encampment. The ground was hard and cold, and there was no fire to ward off the chill. They huddled close together for warmth and protection. Although they could not see them, the captives were aware of the hostile eyes of the Indians watching them.

Eventually the youngest children slept, but fear and aching fatigue made slumber impossible for the others.

"Sleep, child," Mary's mother whispered to her. "Sleep if you can." Mary was frightened, but Ma's gentle strength gave her comfort. Her eyes closed and she slept.

Dawn broke, and the Indians roused the prisoners to begin the march again. At sunrise they were halted and given food from the supply of provisions taken from the Jemisons' home. Everyone ate hungrily. Everyone, that is, except Pa. No amount of urging could get him to accept a morsel.

"Tom. Tom Jemison!" his wife said in a soft, firm voice. "Eat. You must keep up your strength."

Mr. Jemison stared blankly at his wife and moved his head away from the food she held before his mouth.

"Do you hear me?" she asked. "Please, Tom. You must eat something."

Silently he refused. Mary could not bear to see him look so hopeless.

Again the march resumed. Shortly before the sun reached its noon-day high, the party passed a small fort. It lay in ruins.

"That's Fort Canagojigge," Mr. Jemison gasped. He spoke the words flatly, as if his last hopes of rescue were gone. They were the only words he had uttered since the raiding party had descended upon his family the morning before. They were the last words Mary would ever hear him speak.

All day the march continued. Mrs. Mann twisted her ankle and could scarcely keep up with the rest of the party. Mary's mother carried the baby for her after that, and Mary and Betsey helped the smaller children. Everyone's feet were blistered and bruised. Angry red welts from the whip streaked the legs of most of them. They stumbled more often. Each step became more painful than the one before, but they knew the Indians would show no mercy to anyone who fell behind. Not knowing their destination or their ultimate fate made the miles even more unbearable.

Finally, toward sundown, the party came to the edge of a vast swampland thickly covered with evergreens. They were led for some distance through dark thickets of young hemlock before the Indians chose a spot to camp.

The captives were given bread and meat for their supper, but Mary did not want any. What was the use? Any moment the hatchet might fall upon them. Mary prayed that if it happened, it would happen swiftly. She had heard about Indian tortures, and she shivered.

Once again Mrs. Jemison urged everyone to eat.

"You'll need your strength," she said to Mary. Mr. Jemison, hopelessly lost in his deep melancholy, refused again to eat or to speak.

Though she was too weary to be hungry and too frightened to swallow comfortably, Mary ate in obedience to her mother. She ate slowly and without relish, chewing each mouthful absently until it dissolved into a tasteless nothingness.

When she had finished the food that had been given to her, one of the Indians came to the spot where she sat. He carried a pair of moccasins, which he set down beside him. Squatting down, he began to remove Mary's shoes, slowly and gently, with a display of ceremony.

Mary trembled. A painful sob escaped from her mother, who was sitting beside her. "Mary, my little Mary," she said, "I fear that we shall be parted now."

Mary began to cry softly.

"Hush, child," her mother said gently. "Don't cry. It appears that your life is going to be spared. The Indians have singled you out from the rest of us and are giving you Indian moccasins so you can go on with them. I am sure the rest of us will"—she faltered—"will not see you again."

Mary's mother paused. She drew in a sharp breath and then swallowed hard before she said the next words. "If your life is spared, child, have courage. Don't try to escape from the Indians. They will torture you—even kill you—if you try to leave them."

"But, Ma," Mary interrupted, "what about you and Pa?" She looked at Thomas Jemison, still bent in silence.

Mrs. Jemison ignored the question. She squeezed her daughter's hand tightly. "Remember your own name," she went on. "And remember the name of your father and mother. Be careful not to forget the English tongue. Most of all, child, remember your prayers. Say them often. Be a good girl, Mary. God will bless you."

Mary's face was wet with tears. The Indian had finished putting the moccasins on her feet. He had waited silently, almost politely, for the mother to finish speaking to her daughter. Then he rose and led Mary from the group. Her mother called after her, "Don't cry, Mary—don't cry, my child. God will bless you! Farewell—farewell!"

Five

At the same moment that Mary's shoes were being exchanged for Indian moccasins, similar moccasins were being placed on another of the captives. It was nine-year-old Will Mann, who was about the same size as Mary, though almost six years younger. He and Mary were led away from their families, one on each side of the tall Indian warrior, who held them by the hand as he took them farther into the swamp. After they had traveled a considerable distance through the dense undergrowth, the Indian stopped and motioned for them to lie down. He stretched out near them and made them to understand that they were to sleep.

Sleep? Mary's heart pounded. How could she sleep! How could she hope to sleep ever again! What would happen to her now? What was happening to Ma and Pa? And to Betsey and Robert and little Matthew? Would she ever see them again?

Mary wept. The grief-stricken boy beside her wept, too. After a while, as Mary remembered Ma's courage, her sobs lessened. Will rolled closer to her. "We must escape," he whispered. There was panic in his voice.

"No," Mary said firmly. "We'd be caught."

"We're already caught," Will answered. "We must try."

"Try to sleep," Mary said, echoing the advice Ma had given the night before.

"I can't," he said. "I don't want to stay with the Indians. I want to go back to my mother."

Throughout the night Will urged again and again that they try to escape. Although Mary wanted to get away from the Indians as desperately as he did, she knew Ma's warning held truth. Nevertheless, she couldn't help thinking about it. Could they get away without being caught? Would it be possible to find their way back through the trackless forests? What would they do for food? Suppose they encountered a bear or a wild bobcat. And what would the Indians do to them if they caught them again?

Mary shuddered. There was no satisfaction in the answers to the questions she forced herself to consider. Eventually she fell asleep pondering the likelihood of their getting away safely.

The next morning they awoke to a babble of voices. The four Frenchmen and the rest of the Indians had rejoined them, but there were no signs of the other captives. Mary tried not to think what must have happened to them. Instinctively she knew that they had been killed. She was sure of it, but she tried hard not to believe it.

She stifled the sobs that arose within her as she thought about her family. The Indians gave her meat and bread. It was a relief to be doing something, even if it were just chewing. She had no appetite, but she ate. So did Will. Then the march began.

Now the party moved through the forest at a pace faster than before. There was no question but that the men were in great haste. Mary's slim legs flew over the forest floor. She knew better than to complain. She knew, too, that she'd better not fall behind.

One of the Indians stayed a short distance behind the rest of the procession. Using a long staff, he straightened up the grass and weeds that had been trampled down to make the trail look untraveled. No one could tell that people had passed over it recently, and Mary's hope of rescue diminished.

The westward trail they followed led endlessly uphill. Then, after an exhausting climb, it wound downhill. Mary was vaguely aware that they were crossing the great mountains that separated white civilization from the unknown wilderness. At times the procession left the trail, only to rejoin it again farther on. A rescue party would have great difficulty tracking them.

Except for occasional patches of sunlight, it was shadowy in the pine forests through which the trail

led. In the early afternoon of the third day, the shadows blackened as thunder rumbled overhead. Soon the dark clouds released their heavy burden, and rain pommeled through the trees. Mary's blond hair lay flat and wet against her head. Her sodden dress clung uncomfortably to her cold body, and her moccasins squished with every step. On and on through the wet forest she plunged—uphill and downhill, never stopping, never resting.

The Indians made a shelter of boughs when they encamped late that afternoon. They built a large fire, and Mary dried herself and her clothing before it. How good the warmth felt! She and Will were given food, and then they were ignored. They stretched out on the ground to sleep. Mary's legs ached, but after a while she began to relax and to look with curiosity at her captors, who were huddled over their packs.

Suddenly Mary clamped her hand over her mouth to silence a scream that rose in her throat. The Indians were drawing from buckskin bags several freshly taken scalps.

At the sight of the bloody scalps, Mary buried her face into the blanket. If only she could blot out the horror they evoked. For a moment she felt deathly sick.

Finally she forced herself to look up and identify the scalps. The color and length of the hair on each one matched exactly the hair of one of the people left behind the night before. Especially there was no mistaking Ma's red hair. Silent tears rolled down Mary's face as she watched the Indians proceed with the grim business of curing the scalps. A sob shook her as she thought of her mother and father whom she would never see again. Mary cried uncontrollably until she could cry no more.

Her grief and sorrow became mixed with feelings of disgust and contempt for the Indians. No wonder people called them savages! Though she knew of the barbaric practice of scalping and had heard that the French government paid bounty for enemy scalps, seeing the scalps of her own family being prepared as war trophies was an act so horrible that Mary could find no words for her rage.

She lay awake far into the night. Later, when the warriors had finished their work, they spoke to her. By using pantomime and by drawing simple pictures in the dirt, they explained that they had killed the others only because they were being followed and could not travel with so many people fast enough to avoid being overtaken. There was a curious gentleness in the manner of their explanation. At dawn, they said, they must travel even faster to evade the pursuers.

The next day's march was hard for Mary and Will. That night they camped in the open without shelter and without a fire.

A freezing drizzle fell the following morning. All day long it alternated between snow and rain. Mary became numb with the cold. She stumbled along, running most of the time—as much to keep from freezing as to keep up with the fast-moving warriors. She paid no attention to the landscape through which she passed. All her thoughts were focused upon the need to keep moving. She was completely exhausted. Her clothing was drenched. She knew that if she stopped even for a moment, she would not be able to go on.

By the time they halted to make camp that night, the snow was falling fast. Mary felt as if she would never be able to walk again. The Indians made a fire and put together a shelter of boughs. As the heat of the fire warmed her, Mary felt the numbness slowly leave her body. Finally she stopped shivering. She ate food the Indians gave her, and then she slept. When she awakened the next morning, she felt somewhat better. Because the snow had continued to fall throughout the night, the Indians chose to remain in their shelter until the storm ceased.

The following day another war party joined them at their encampment. There were six Indians and a captive white man. The Indians were acquainted with one another. They were all Shawnees.

Mary quickened at the sight of the young white man, hoping he might know the way back over the mountains or be helpful in planning an escape. She realized soon, however, that he was in no condition to escape. He was as tired and discouraged as she was—perhaps more so. He slumped to the ground and sat helplessly with his head propped upon his hands. He was too weak even to talk.

Some of the warriors left camp to hunt for food. They brought back a deer, which, after skinning and preparing, they roasted whole over the fire. They shared the meat and what bread was left with the captives.

On the morning of the third day in the encampment, both groups resumed a westward march together. The leaders did not appear to be in such great haste as before, and the Indian who had previously followed behind erasing their trail now made no effort to obliterate the signs of their passing. Mary realized dimly that the change to a less hurried pace could only mean that the Indians felt safe from being overtaken by a search party.

Gradually the trail widened into a well-worn path of hard-packed earth. It emerged from the thick woodlands and followed high ground above the winding Monongahela River. That afternoon, after following the riverbank for a considerable distance, they came to a fort built on a point of land where the Monongahela and the Allegheny Rivers merge to form the great Ohio.

"Fort Duquesne," the white man whispered furtively to Mary.

Mary thought hard. Duquesne? Where had she

heard the funny-sounding name? Then she remembered. She had heard a Marsh Creek neighbor telling Pa some time ago about the fortifications the French were building far to the west of the mountains—two weeks' journey away, or more. The forts were built for military defense of French claims to the Ohio and Mississippi valley lands, and Fort Duquesne guarded the strategic position at the grand forks of the Ohio. But that was an impossible distance from Marsh Creek. The young man must be mistaken.

The travelers halted outside the walls of the fort. Mary stared at the gray wooden stockade that surrounded it. Directly ahead was a blockhouse built into the wall. She wondered if there were muskets trained on them from the small openings near its top. She was glad to be at the fort, however, because it had been built and occupied by white men. She hoped it might mean freedom from Indian captivity.

Before entering the fort, two of the Indians began cutting Will Mann's hair. First, using a sharp knife, they cut off all the hair that grew down onto his neck. Then they shaved his head with a sharp flint stone, leaving only a rounded crest of hair like the scalp lock of the Shawnee. Several times Mary saw Will grimace and jerk his head in pain as the rough stone scraped away bits of skin along with his hair. Though he did not cry out, Mary knew it was a painful ordeal. Next they did the same thing to the young white man.

The oldest-looking of the Indians beckoned Mary to him and began to untangle her hair with a crude comb made of bone. He worked gently until her hair was free from snarls and burrs. When he had finished, Mary's long golden locks hung in silken strands below her shoulders. Some of the Indians stared at her. Mary remained grimly silent and expressionless throughout the procedure.

Then from a hollow gourd, the Indian daubed a sticky red substance onto Mary's face. He painted similar designs on the faces of the other two captives.

The sight of Will's pale shaven head and his red painted face made Mary turn away. He looked so raw and plucked. His scared little face and his disheveled clothes added to the pathetic image. He was thinner than he had been when they were captured. She knew she must look equally miserable, and for the first time she noticed how tattered and ragged her clothes had become. She felt tears welling up within her again, but this time she held them back.

At dusk she and Will and the young man were escorted inside the fort by their abductors and led through a courtyard to a small lean-to log hut built along the inside of the wall. The Indians motioned for them to go inside. Then the door was bolted from the outside, and they were left alone.

Six

The only light in the crude shelter into which the captives had been shut filtered through a small opening in the wall near the ceiling. When Mary's eyes adjusted to the dimness, she saw that the room was bare except for a pile of hay stacked in one corner. Its scent lay heavy in the air.

Young Will was trembling. Mary knew that his shaven head must still burn fiercely where the skin had been scraped by the flint stone. He had not fully recovered from the fear of being scalped while the Indians were shaving off his hair. Now he shivered violently and appeared near collapse.

Mary piled armloads of hay into the shape of a pallet. Then she made Will lie down on it. She sat on the floor beside him and cushioned his head on her lap in the folds of her skirt.

"It's all right, Will," she said softly, trying to comfort him. "Your head won't hurt so much tomorrow. Please try to sleep. Sleep will make you feel better."

He smiled at her weakly and closed his eyes in

obedience. A closeness had developed between them since the day they had been taken from their families. Besides sharing the ordeal of the arduous trek with the Indians, Mary and Will each represented to the other an irreplaceable link with the past.

After a while Will fell into a fitful sleep. Mary stayed quietly beside him. It was good to have him to comfort. Somehow, worrying about someone else helped to ease the strain. She could not keep her thoughts away from the gnawing question of what would happen to them next.

"He seems calmer now," the other prisoner whispered, nodding toward Will.

"I'm worried about him," Mary said. "I'm worried about all of us. I wish I knew what was going to happen to us."

"Aye, and so do I," the young man said in a voice heavy with anxiety. "I hope we won't be forced to run the gantlet." He shook his head woefully as he spoke.

Remembering stories she had heard of Indian torture, Mary shuddered.

"I heard once," the young man said, "that when the Indians paint their prisoners' faces with red designs, it means they're planning to adopt them." He paused. Then he added ominously, "Black paint means death."

Unconsciously Mary drew her hand down one side of her face and looked numbly at the crimson smudges on her fingertips. Although the color confirmed what

54

she already knew, the ray of hope was small comfort.

Neither Mary nor the young man could sleep. Hope alternating with despair kept Mary tensed and wary throughout the long black night.

When the first morning light came, the Indians un-bolted the door and motioned the captives into the courtyard. Will and the young man were given over at once to a group of French soldiers, who led them away. Will looked back over his shoulder at Mary. His wistful face wore a look of deep misery. She wondered if she would ever see him again—suspecting, even then, that she would not.

Her captors left, and Mary felt conspicuous standing alone in the empty courtyard. She did not know what to do with herself or what she was expected to do. They had not indicated that she should go back inside the cabin. While she was wondering whether she should return to it or stay where she was, a bugle sounded. Instinctively Mary stepped back toward the cabin as three French soldiers bounded toward her, yawning, stretching, and rubbing sleep from their eyes. They walked past, taking no notice of her. A skinny brown dog followed after them. Next, an officer hurried past wearing the most elegant uniform she had ever seen. Its white coat buttoned over a powder blue waistcoat above fitted breeches, lace cuffs flared at his wrists, and gold lace adorned his hat.

Then two agreeable-looking Indian women padded

into the compound and paused across from where Mary stood. They stared at her with such solemnity that she felt obliged to look away. She could feel their eyes upon her for what seemed to be a long time, and she could hear them whispering. She looked toward them again in time to see them nod to each other as if in agreement. Then slowly and deliberately, with measured steps, they approached her.

Mary stood motionless while they circled around her, moving closer to look at her in frank appraisal from every angle and from head to toe. Mary's heart stopped its fearful pounding as she began to sense a cordiality in their attitude and a friendliness in their inspection.

Tactfully she made a return appraisal. Both were pleasant-looking; one of them was probably not many years older than she was. The younger was the more comely of the two. She was slim and straight, whereas her companion was stocky and somewhat stooped. The features of their dark-skinned faces were similar— prominent high cheekbones, small hawk-bridged noses, and dark brown eyes. Each wore her long black hair pulled back from her face and tied at the nape of the neck with a leather thong. They were both dressed in leggings and tunics of deerskin. Only the embroidery on their tunics distinguished one outfit from the other.

The older one stared especially long and intently at Mary's hair. Finally she reached out timidly to touch it. The gesture made Mary smile at her. The woman smiled, too. There was a kindliness in her eyes. It was the first feeling of warmth Mary had felt in so long that she was saddened when both women moved off silently, leaving her alone again.

A short while later the two women returned in the company of the six Shawnee Indians who had taken Mary from her home and brought her to Fort Duquesne. As they had done once before, her abductors talked to her with a combination of sign language, gesturing, and simple stick drawings in the dirt.

She was to go with the two women, they explained. The women were sisters of the Seneca tribe, and she was being *given* to them now as *their* captive. They had accepted her as bounty to replace their brother who had been killed in battle. According to Indian custom, the family of a slain warrior could claim either a prisoner or an enemy scalp.

The warriors accompanied Mary and her new owners out of the fort and to the river's edge. One of the women slid into a small elm-bark canoe and motioned for Mary to follow. It wobbled from side to side as she settled herself in its center, rigid and tense for fear the canoe would capsize and dump them all into the water. She was not afraid of the water, but she was in terror of doing anything that might anger her new owners. She held her breath as the older sister got in. Instead of swaying dangerously as it had when

Mary got in, the canoe remained steady and upright. The woman settled herself into the stern and, with a swift motion, shoved the boat from the shore with her paddle.

The six Shawnees had already embarked in a larger canoe and were paddling downstream just ahead. The scarfaced warrior stood near the stern raising a long pole into the air. Mary watched intently as he held it high, supporting it on his shoulder. He carried it as if it were a banner. Fastened to it, like trophies flying in the wind, were scalps. Again Mary recognized them. The grim reminders brought fresh floods of memory to her, and for a long while she remained lost in grief.

Who would take care of her now? And who would she turn to for comfort or help? True, she was almost grown up. Girls in the frontier colonies often married at fifteen. But Mary didn't feel at all grown up just now. She wanted her mother and father and the familiar and good things that had been a part of her life with the family at Marsh Creek.

The Indian sisters appeared not to notice Mary's despair. The one in the stern of the canoe kept a silent watch over her, observing the sobs that shook her with a look that indicated understanding—perhaps even sympathy. She made no effort, however, to comfort her.

While the canoe slid quietly over miles of the winding river, Mary remained lost in sorrow, unaware of her surroundings and unconcerned about her destination. It was as if all the things that had happened these past nine days had happened to someone else—not to her. It was as if she were only having a bad dream about being an Indian captive.

Gradually, as the sun rose higher in the morning sky, Mary's thoughts of the past changed slowly to an awareness of the present. It was beautiful along the broad Ohio. She inhaled the new spring smells. Fragrant red-bud blossoms contrasted with the yellow-green of the uncurling willow fronds. Often the river separated itself into two streams around small islands. The banks of the river rose abruptly into steep cliffs of yellow clay. In places the cliffs gave way to lowlands where new green foliage marched to the edge of the water. Farther along, sandy beaches narrowly paralled the water's edge. Then the river wound again in giant bends around tall, rocky palisades that rose spectacularly toward the sky.

As Mary became aware of the landscape through which she was passing, she began to be curious about where she was and where the Indian women were taking her. She wondered what life with the Indians might be like. Would she be their servant or would they treat her as a member of their family?

After a while Mary realized that, for the first time since the Indians had swooped down upon the Jemison farm over a week ago, she had stopped being afraid. Death had hovered over her so closely since her capture that her freedom from terror was a surprising sensation. She did not know at what moment fear had left her. She only knew that it was gone. It did not matter now whether the Indians treated her as family or as slave. She was alive!

Mary lifted her eyes and watched the scene before her. It was not a dream, and it was not happening to some other girl. It was she, Mary Jemison, who was an Indian captive, heading toward an unknown fate. But now she was not afraid, and that made all the difference.

She could wait patiently—weeks, maybe even months, if necessary—hopeful of finding a way to escape from the Indians.

Seven

Hour after hour the small canoe skimmed downstream along the winding Ohio River. Mary had not attempted to determine the direction in which it was carrying her. Farther away from Marsh Creek, she suspected. The river rounded so many bends that keeping track was impossible. Now in the sunless early evening, there was no way of telling direction, even had she tried.

Dusk replaced the hazy twilight, and the air grew chill. On and on they traveled, the sisters dipping their paddles with a steady rhythm. Mary could not help admiring their stamina. They had kept pace all day with the Shawnee warriors in the larger canoe just ahead, plying their paddles skillfully hour upon hour without complaint or murmur of fatigue.

A low-pitched whistle, from the direction of the Shawnee's canoe startled Mary's senses into focus. It was followed by a similar signal made by the sister in the stern of the canoe. Moments later, the little craft turned and headed toward the shore.

Upon reaching the edge, the Seneca women leaped from the canoe and disappeared into the underbrush, leaving Mary alone and stunned by the abruptness of their departure. It was not clear to her whether she was expected to stay where she was or to follow them. She looked around for the larger canoe of the Shawnees. It was hard to see anything distinctly along the shoreline, but she was sure the Shawnees had not landed. Apparently the whistle she had heard from their boat had been a signal of farewell.

Mary waited. Soon she heard rustling sounds from the underbrush into which the sisters had disappeared. Had they come back angry because she had not followed on their heels? As they emerged from the thicket, Mary could see that each of them was carrying a bundle. Judging from the short span of time that they had been gone, Mary reckoned that they must have obtained the bundles nearby.

The woman lifted Mary out of the canoe and began to unfasten her dress. One by one they removed her ragged clothes from her body and threw them into the river. At the sight of her dress floating downstream, Mary winced as if struck by pain. She lurched forward, hoping to rescue it, but the sisters held her fast. The clothes were Mary's last tangible links with home and her family. She wanted desperately to fetch them back —especially the dress. Ma had made it for her, and even though it was no longer fit for wearing, it was suddenly more precious to her than ever before. Once it had been new and pretty—its fabric a crisp blue and gray mixture of homespun linen and wool that her mother had woven on the big loom that occupied so much space in the Jemison home. Even the linen thread had been made from flax grown in the fields at home. Mary remembered how she and Betsey had loved wiggling their toes in the soft earth when they helped Pa with the springtime weeding among the flax plants.

Mary stood naked at the water's edge while the sisters bathed her. Their motions were quick and gentle, but the cold water against her skin made her shiver. Then they dressed her in clothing they had brought. Mary wrinkled her nose. It was Indian clothing made of animal skins. How strange it smelled! But the deerskin leggings felt soft against her legs, and the skirt that went over them warmed her. A tunic hung gracefully from a yoke decorated with a gay embroidery. Mary learned later that the embroidery was of dyed porcupine quills. At the gown's hemline was soft, deep fringe.

The elder sister handed Mary a pair of moccasins and indicated that she was to put them on. They, too, were soft and new. Mary slipped them on while the sisters chattered happily to each other, apparently

pleased that the garments were such a good fit. Quickly, but with obvious pleasure, they combed her hair with a comb made of bone, and they both fussed over arranging the long strands into two thick braids.

Then, with low chuckling sounds and nods of agreement, they led Mary through the rough, prickly underbrush until they emerged upon a narrow trail that ran alongside a shallow creek. A short distance more and they arrived at the site of an Indian settlement. Quietly and without greeting anyone, they led Mary into one of the lodges and made her sit upon the dirt floor in its center.

Almost immediately women of the village filed into the lodge and surrounded Mary. Not knowing what behavior was expected of her, she sat motionless with her head slightly bowed. Then, some moments later, the muffled shuffling of moccasined feet upon the dirt floor stopped. Mary inquisitively raised her eyes.

A great many Indian women had crowded around her. They were of all ages, shapes, and sizes. Some were young and pretty; others were toothless and bent with age. Some of them stared at her sternly; others pointed their fingers at her. One or two reached out to touch her hair—so pale and silken in contrast to the black coarseness of their own.

Mary was terrified. She wondered what they were going to do to her. Had she survived the hardships of the long forced march and the suspense of the past week only to become a torture victim? Her mind groped for a reasonable explanation that might blot out the new fear, but her efforts were distracted by strange noises being made by the Indian women. She looked about her in disbelief. They were crying! Tears poured down their faces, and they were moaning and wailing as if their grief would never end.

Weary and now perplexed, Mary tried to find a meaning. Were they crying because they felt sorry for her? Because she was an orphan? Or—because of something that was going to happen to her?

For several long minutes the women appeared to be in a genuine state of grief, wringing their hands, their faces distorted with weeping. Altogether it was a dismal sight, and the sound of their wailing was deafening.

Such a noise would wake the dead, Mary thought. Behind the giddy observation lay a truth she did not suspect. The wailing women were, in fact, trying to commune with the spirit-world. They were attempting to evoke the name-spirit of a young warrior—the brother of the two sisters—who had been slain. It was part of the Indian adoption ceremony as they sought to bestow his name-spirit upon Mary.

After a period of grieving for the dead brother, one of the women began to recite in a sing-song chant:

"Our brother, alas, he is dead.
He died on the field of the slain.
With glory he fell.

"His spirit went up to the land of his fathers.
With joy they received him.
Oh, friends he is happy!"

Mary, of course, could not understand the meaning of the Indian words. They were chanted in a high-pitched tone. The women expressed the mood of the chant by swaying their bodies and shaking their heads and by rolling their eyes and wringing their hands. It was as if they were acting out a play.

Gradually the chanting grew lighter in tone. The women dried their tears. Smiles replaced their sad, tearful grimace, and they looked at Mary with expressions of welcome, saying:

"Deh-ge-wa-nus has come. Let us receive her with joy. She is handsome and pleasant. Oh, she is our sister. Gladly we welcome her here in the place of our brother."

When the ceremony was over, Mary Jemison had been legally adopted by the Seneca Indians into the family of the two sisters who had taken her as their prisoner from Fort Duquesne. Hereafter she would be treated with the same high regard accorded to women of the Iroquois tribes. Her Indian name was Deh-ge-wa-nus, which meant "Two Voices Falling."

Eight

Life in the Indian village was placid and unhurried. A number of the Indians went out of their way to speak a gentle word to Mary. Even though she did not know the meaning of the words, she understood the friendliness behind them. Some of the Indians helped her when she seemed uncertain in her tasks. One by one, the gutteral sounds of their language became distinguishable, and Mary began to understand the meaning of words. The sisters showed great pleasure when she tried to speak to them, and they encouraged her to learn new words.

Occasionally she would lapse into English. At such times the women were scornful. They wanted her to forget her native language and to become entirely Indian. Mary remembered Ma's warning not to forget her English speech and not to forget her prayers, but there was little opportunity for using English. Even though she tried to repeat her prayers each night, she often fell asleep before finishing them.

The prayer most often in her thoughts was that she

might return home to Marsh Creek. In daydreams and in her last waking thoughts at night, she pictured her home and her family, and she yearned to return.

About forty Indians altogether dwelt in the small village in a cluster of low huts. An open space nearby, cleared of trees and underbrush, served as farmland for their crops. The most important was corn, and it was planted and tended by the women and the children. Beans and squash and sometimes pumpkins grew in between the cornstalks. Mary found helping in the fields pleasant; she had always liked to help Pa and her brothers. Here the fields were not well cleared or nearly so well tended as Pa's had been. But that was because the Indians moved their villages from time to time. When game became scarce in the surrounding forests or when the soil would no longer support the same crops season after season, the inhabitants of an Indian village moved to a new site.

The interior of the bark-covered hut in which Mary lived with her adopted sisters required very little housekeeping. Its only furnishings were low pole platforms covered with animal skins, which served them for beds. A smell of grease and smoke clung to the bark walls. Fresh air entered only through a small opening, where a flap of deerhide took the place of a door. The heavy odor inside was offensive to Mary, and it sometimes made her gag. Often she was forced to breathe through her mouth to avoid smelling it.

Each morning Mary began her chores by bringing wood and fresh water to the hut. Inside, the sisters squatted before the fire preparing food for the morning meal. There was a hole in the roof of the hut for the smoke to escape, but there was no chimney, and smoke often filled the entire hut. Mary was glad for her morning chores, which took her into the clear, fresh air outside. After the meal she carried their few cooking utensils to the stream to rinse them—a hominy block and pestle, a small kettle, two knives, and a few vessels of bark and wood. On some days she went with other Indian women and girls to gather berries and nuts. Of all her tasks, she most enjoyed caring for the younger children while their mothers were busy.

Her most tedious chore was pounding corn for the day's food supply. Corn was the most important food in the Indians' diet and the basis for most of their meals. They ate fresh corn-on-the-cob, roasted or broiled. Sometimes they made a thick pottage from dried corn, which they ground with a pestle in a wooden mortar. They added meat or smoked fish to the pottage for variety. Often they preferred a thin corn soup.

Their flat bread, made from kneaded corn flour and water, was shaped into little cakes and wrapped in leaves before baking in hot ashes. Sometimes they mixed berries with the flour for a new flavor. Mary yearned for the light yeasty loaves of bread that Ma used to bake in the hearthside oven back home. By

71

comparison, Indian bread was tasteless and flat, but eventually she became used to its flavor and even liked it.

Occasionally Mary was sent along on short hunting trips to help carry home heavy loads of game or fur pelts on her back. The Indians taught her to support them with a tumpline—a flat strap that pressed across her forehead and fastened to either side of the load on her back. It was necessary for her to lean forward in order to balance the heavy load. In time, she grew used to the pressure against her forehead. All Seneca woman used the tumpline—mothers to carry babies on their backs in a cradleboard, girls to haul bulky loads of firewood, women to tote baskets of corn from the fields or maple sirup from the sugar camps.

When the men of the village were not off hunting, they spent their time fishing, felling trees, clearing more land, repairing their bark houses, and making canoes and weapons.

Mary learned to distinguish roots and plants that were safe to eat from similar-looking plants whose poisons could bring on swift and painful death. She learned of forest signposts that enabled warriors to find their way home from great distances. She watched young boys being taught to identify sounds and scents until they could use their noses and ears with almost as much skill as their eyes.

Mary saw the Indian men relax with laughter and

gaiety in the company of their families when they returned from long hunting forays. They played games and told stories and enjoyed singing and dancing at festivals. Mary watched from the shadows as they frolicked happily. Until she had come to live with them, she had imagined that Indians were always somber and stern.

As the spring days of Mary's early captivity lengthened into summer, her understanding of the Indian language increased. She learned then that the Seneca encampment where she was being held captive was situated along the banks of the River Ohio, deep within Ohio territory (not far from what is now Steubenville, Ohio). She learned, too, that this was not actually the homeland of the Senecas. They belonged to a large and powerful tribe whose territory extended across present-day New York State between Cayuga Lake and the banks of the Genesee River. The Senecas were part of the great Iroquois League, and their fearsome warriors had invaded lands of less powerful tribes and conquered them. In this way the Senecas had established settlements in the Ohio territory to guard their fur trade and to keep enemy Indians from hunting there. Long ago, before conquest by the Senecas, these lands had belonged to other Indian tribes.

Mary was told that the proud and fierce Senecas were called People of the High Hill. She listened wide-eyed while an elderly warrior repeated the ancient legend of how his ancestors had emerged from a rocky hill near Canandaigua Lake only to be beheaded by a giant serpent. Not until a brave warrior destroyed the monstrous beast were his people saved from total annihilation. The Senecas believed the rocks at the base of the hill to be the petrified skulls of their ancestors, which the serpent disgorged when his wounded and dying body tumbled downhill to the edge of the lake.

Mary measured time by the growth of the corn. When summer had passed into autumn, activity within the village increased. The men busied themselves repairing canoes, chipping flint, fletching arrows, and making bows. The women harvested and prepared the corn. They loaded it onto horses and into canoes. Then the villagers, Mary and the sisters among them, moved downriver to the spot where the Scioto joins the broad Ohio River. Here they set about establishing a winter camp.

The forests around the new campsite were rich with game. Often Mary traveled deep into the woodland with the hunters to assist them in carrying back elk and deer. The sisters taught her to preserve meat by cutting it into thin strips and then drying the strips. Ma had done this, she remembered. She had called it "jerked meat." Mary helped the women prepare the animal hides, too. The best ones were set aside for marketing.

From the sisters she learned the importance of the fur trade. Until the white men had come to this land, they told her, the Indians had been rather primitive creatures, eking out their daily existence by relying on nature and on the Great Spirit. Then the white men had arrived in winged vessels from across the sea. They brought magic treasures—flashing mirrors with which to signal or in which to see one's likeness reflected; soft pliable cloth in vivid colors never before seen by the Indians, cloth more supple than even the softest of doeskins; and tools of iron, strong, well-shaped tools such as the Indians had never dreamed existed, that eased their labors and did not break. Their own crude axes were of stone. Even the heads of their war clubs and the short-handled hoe used by their women to cultivate crops had been chiseled from stone, sometimes only from wood. Indian tools were dull by comparison. They broke easily and took long tedious hours to repair.

Once the Indians had tried the white men's inventions, the sisters explained, they could not do without them. They did not know how to make them, but they wanted them. The white men wanted the fur pelts of the beaver and the otter, and would trade their treasures for them. But the white men were scaring away the animals by encroaching upon lands belonging to the Indians. Farm by farm and fort by fort, the French and the English had overrun Indian hunting grounds. Now the French and the English were fighting each other for ownership of land—land that belonged to neither of them! Moreover, the sisters added indignantly, the double-dealing French and the land-grabbing English wanted the Indians to help them battle one another for the land!

Mary listened attentively. Now, for the first time, she began to understand the conflict from the point of view of the Indians.

Nine

Throughout the winter of the year 1759, Mary remained with the Indians at their new camp. The warriors were away most of the time, returning periodically with game and furs. Sometimes they came with fresh scalps dangling from their belts.

When spring arrived and they returned to their Ohio River village, Mary helped prepare the fields for planting. She hoed the ground into small hillocks, and her sisters followed behind planting the precious corn seed in the mounds of dirt.

A few days after the planting, they told Mary that she would accompany them and others of the village on a journey. Obediently Mary helped pack the necessary food and blankets into the canoes, and at dawn they paddled away from the riverbanks. When night fell, they beached their canoes and made camp atop the steep walls of the embankment along the river.

The next morning Mary was startled with the familiarity of the panorama seen from the hilltop encampment. Far below swirled the waters of two mighty

rivers that came together to form a single waterway of great breadth. A small fort stood on the point of land where the two rivers met. A flag fluttered from one of the fort's bastions. Mary knew she had been there before, but this was not the strange flag she remembered seeing there a year ago. This was an English flag, and the fort itself appeared different, too. She frowned in puzzlement. "Why are the Indians bringing me here?" she asked herself. Slowly at first, but with growing excitement, her mind began to seethe with questions.

From snatches of talk heard among the Indians during the past weeks, Mary knew that great numbers of English soldiers had come into the Ohio country. Perhaps the English soldiers had forced the French to leave the fort at the forks of the river. If this was true and if the Indians were coming to an English-held fort, it could only be to talk peace.

Could the sisters be returning her to her own people? She looked toward the Seneca women for a sign that might supply an answer, but their expressionless faces told her nothing.

Mary's excitement grew. Finally, with as much calm as she could muster, she asked the sisters, "Are you taking me back to the white people?"

"No," the older one replied. "You are part of our family. We shall not give you away. We have come to discuss trade with the English. Our warriors want peace."

79

Mary lowered her eyes so they would not see her disappointment.

When the gates of the stockade were opened to them later that morning, the Indians of Mary's village were ushered by red-coated soldiers toward a meeting area. Mary lagged behind, feasting her eyes on the details of the buildings and the splendid uniforms the soldiers wore. She walked toward a group of white people clustered near the gates. Seeing the deerskin-clad girl with yellow hair and blue eyes, the white people surrounded her and began to ask questions.

"What is your name?" one asked.

"Who are you?" another piped.

"Where did you come from?" asked another. The questions were coming faster than Mary could answer.

"How long have you been with the Indians?"

"Where are your parents?"

Mary began to answer excitedly. "I am Dehge-wanus," she said. She stopped and began again. "My name is Mary Jemison." Her words came with hesitation. She had not forgotten the English language, but she had not used it for a long time, and she spoke haltingly.

The white people wanted to know more about Mary's capture and captivity than they had time to find out. Before the conversation had progressed beyond the exchange of a few sentences, Mary felt the tight grip of strong hands upon her arms pulling her away from the knot of white people. Each holding one of her arms, the sisters led her from the fort in such haste that Mary's feet barely skimmed the ground.

They whisked Mary back to the river and into a canoe. And just as quickly they shoved off from shore and paddled hurriedly to the opposite bank. Once across the river, one of them hastened up the steep incline and returned moments later carrying the few possessions they had left at the campsite. Then they paddled the canoe away from the fort back down the broad and winding Ohio River. According to the report that Mary gave to her biographer years later, the sisters were so afraid of losing her or of her being taken away from them that they never stopped paddling until they arrived at their village.

Days later when the other Indians returned, Mary learned that soon after the sisters had taken her from the fort, the white people had crossed the river in pursuit. They had asked many questions at the Indian encampment concerning her whereabouts. They tried to learn where she had been taken or where she was hidden. Only after much searching and questioning had they returned to Fort Pitt, as the English now called the fort, disappointed that they had missed the opportunity of returning a captive to her people.

To Mary, of course, it was as if she had been taken prisoner all over again. She had begun to adjust to life with the Indians, but coming so close to freedom was a bitter setback. Many weeks of sorrow and grief were to pass before she would forget how close she had been to escaping from captivity.

All summer she worked with the Indians in the cornfields. The sisters treated her with a special kindness. They tried to spare her some of the heavy tasks, but Mary discovered that hard work served to ease the heaviness in her heart. Only by working till she was physically exhausted could she sleep at night without tossing and turning in endless fretting over the missed opportunity. The work made her strong. Her small slender body acquired a toughness and strength that was belied by her fragile appearance.

That autumn after the harvest, the Indians again journeyed downriver to winter hunting grounds. Mary spent these months becoming acquainted with Gayen-gontwen and Jiskaakak, two brothers who were part of the Indian family that had adopted her. The brothers, whose English names were Little Billy and Young King, had recently arrived in the Ohio country from their Seneca homeland.

As the third springtime of Mary's captivity approached, the Indians left their winter camp and journeyed upriver to a spot where two rivers empty into the broad Ohio from either side. Here they established a town—cleared the land, planted their crops, and built their huts. They called the place Wiishto. During the summer some Delaware Indians came into the new town with five white prisoners. They were made welcome by the Senecas. The prisoners were all English-speaking people. Mary rejoiced at hearing her native tongue again. One of the prisoners, a girl named Priscilla Ramsay, was soon married to one of the Indian braves.

One day the sisters called Mary to them and told her that she was to live with one of the young Delaware warriors who had come into the town. Mary was dumfounded and not even sure she understood them. She knew, however, that she could not disobey them.

With patience and understanding, the sisters explained to Mary that they had arranged for her to be married to the young Delaware brave called Sheninjee. It was time that their golden-haired sister be married, they said. She was seventeen years old. Most Indian maidens had married by the time they reached Mary's age. In fact, they often married at a younger age. Arrangements for Indian marriages were usually made between the mothers of the bride and the bridegroom, but in the absence of their mother, the sisters told Mary, they had arranged that she become the bride of Sheninjee.

Mary thrust her chin forward stubbornly and stared into space. She did not know what to say. She knew arguing with the women would be useless, and defying them might be dangerous. Mary had already learned that once they had determined upon a course of action, there was no chance of change. Besides, she had lived with the Indians long enough to know that a maiden accepts the husband chosen by her family and that disobedience could result in disownment. She shuddered to think what they might do to her then.

What the sisters said about girls her age being married was, of course, true. She was seventeen—almost eighteen. The second year of her captivity had gone by so rapidly that she was surprised to realize she had been with the Indians so long. She had been rather at ease the past year and had even stopped thinking of escape. She had acquired Indian ways—she walked like an Indian and talked like one, too. She even thought in the language of the Senecas instead of in her native English. She walked with the slightly bent-forward posture that comes from carrying heavy loads on her back with a tumpline stretched tight across her forehead. Her fair skin, though still fairer than any Indian's, was bronzed, and her lithe body was strong and well-coordinated.

While the thought of marriage to Sheninjee was unpleasant to Mary, it did not occur to her to question whether it was marriage or the fact that she was being asked to marry an Indian that troubled her. When she began to sift the reasons for her feelings, she realized that if she had been back home at Marsh Creek, she probably would have been married by now.

A few days later at the conclusion of the simple ceremonies that constitute an Indian marriage, Mary went to live with Sheninjee.

Ten

Mary at first had believed happiness would be impossible as the wife of an Indian. As the summer wore on, however, she discovered that she held her husband in great respect and that she enjoyed their friendship. Sheninjee proudly brought to their hearthside the finest deer and the plumpest wild turkeys. With gentleness and patience, he taught Mary to cook and preserve the meat and to make variations of the corn dishes he had known as a child among the Delawares.

When he teased her for the mistakes she made in her homemaking chores, a softened expression in his dark eyes reassured her of his affection. Mary found herself beginning to trust Sheninjee and to cherish his companionship.

Occasionally in the course of her work, she would recall her parents and her life with them at Marsh Creek. The melancholy of such memories had diminished, however, and was no longer accompanied by feelings of malice toward the Indians. She knew now that Indians were loving and kind toward their friends and families, honest to an astonishing degree, and cruel only to their enemies.

As wife of an Indian, Mary discovered that her life did not differ greatly from the life of a pioneer white woman. In fact, she regarded the Indian way of life as more pleasant and less demanding. Despite the Indian woman's responsibility for raising crops, pounding grain, and maintaining the fire over which she cooked—all men's chores among white families—Mary discovered that she performed these duties with a sense of leisure and enjoyment. There was no master to dictate when the fields must be planted or how they must be hoed and tended. The women worked together happily. Often they helped one another. Their children helped by taking care of the babies or by carrying water from the creek to wet the seedlings. The women chatted and gossiped as they worked.

Thoughts of escaping no longer troubled Mary. She had even stopped thinking of herself as a captive. She had actually found contentment as the wife of Sheninjee, and she loved him.

In the second summer that she and Sheninjee lived at Wiishto, Mary gave birth to a daughter. The baby died after two days. By late summer Mary had ceased to grieve and had regained her strength so that she could accompany the Indians to their winter encampment on the Scioto. About this time her sisters left the

Ohio country to return to the Seneca homeland in western New York.

Early the following spring a son was born to Mary and Sheninjee. They named him Thomas Jemison in memory of Mary's father.

Toward the end of June in the year 1762, Mary and Sheninjee and their tiny blue-eyed son set out by canoe for Fort Pitt, planning to trade the furs Sheninjee had hunted during the past winter for cloth and ammunition. Little Billy and Young King, Mary's brothers, who had come again from the Seneca homeland, traveled with them.

Mary said good-by to her friends of the village with reluctance because she was not sure when she might see them again. She and Sheninjee had discussed continuing on from Fort Pitt to the Genesee country to visit Mary's adopted Seneca family. The sisters had gone there more than a year ago and had urged her repeatedly to come to see them. They sent messages by their brothers, who traveled back and forth at least once each year between Seneca homelands and the Ohio country. It was typical of Indians to think nothing of going off at the slightest provocation on journeys of great length. Often they stayed with friends or relatives an entire year's span in order to travel during the season that suited their convenience.

At the mouth of the Muskingum River, where the

city of Marietta, Ohio, now stands, Sheninjee steered the canoe from the broad Ohio River into the tributary. As they passed a well-known English trading post at the confluence of the rivers, Mary's attention was diverted. Just ahead she saw a sight that sickened her. Three dead bodies were floating downstream toward them. "Look," she said quietly, pointing to the bodies. "There are three of them, and their skins are white."

Sheninjee identified the bodies as those of the three traders who operated the post they had just passed. They had been dead less than a day, he said. He was alarmed at being in the vicinity of the murders for fear that he might be accused of committing them. He turned the canoe about abruptly and paddled rapidly toward the shore near the trading house.

Sheninjee, Young King, and Little Billy cautiously approached the wood structure of the trading post. Mary, with the baby strapped to her back, followed close behind. They found a party of Shawnees in the act of torturing a young white prisoner. Many wounds had already been inflicted upon the young man's body, and the Shawnees were shrieking with laughter at his agony as they kicked him back and forth on the dirt floor.

Mary could not remain silent at the sight of the wounded prisoner having dirt rubbed into his cuts and being whipped unmercifully at the same time. She drew herself tall and straight and confronted the

Shawnees with a dignity that was both arrogant and authoritative despite her small size. "Stop!" she commanded.

The Shawnees grunted at the sound of a woman's voice and looked in that direction. One of them glowered at Mary with narrowed eyes. His eyes widened, however, as he perceived the diminutive blue-eyed, yellow-haired girl glaring back at him. His glance darted sideways to her companions. Two were Senecas —fiercest of all the powerful Iroquois. Little Billy and Young King returned the Shawnee's stare in cold silence. Sheninjee gave him such a hostile look that the Shawnee bully knew better than to provoke him.

Mary seized the opportunity to try to reason with the Shawnees. "The war is over," she pleaded. "There is no excuse for killing him. Set him free."

The Shawnees sneered at her, but they stopped torturing their prisoner. He was already horribly disfigured.

"Go!" Mary said to him in English.

He looked timidly from Mary to her companions, and then he glanced furtively at his captors. The Shawnees, whether stupefied at being given orders by the tiny white woman or afraid of arousing the ire of her companions, shrugged their shoulders and grunted, indicating they had no further use for the prisoner.

"Go that way." Mary pointed toward the direction the young white man should travel, and he fled.

The Shawnees, after admitting to Sheninjee that they had murdered the English traders and looted the post, departed in sullen silence.

Sheninjee, Mary and the baby, Little Billy and Young King paddled upriver some forty miles to a Shawnee town, where they stayed for a few days' rest. Then they moved further upstream to a crossroads Indian town known as Black Bear Town. It is the site of the present Ohio city of Coshocton.

Sheninjee felt it best to spend several days at Black Bear Town to make sure they did not seem to be in haste. He said that their appearance at the trading post so soon after the murders of the owners might draw suspicion upon them. By remaining at the Shawnee town, they would show that they were not running in guilt.

During their stay, another of Mary's Indian brothers arrived from the Seneca homeland. He pleaded with Mary and Sheninjee and his two brothers to journey back with him to the family's home at Little Beard's Town along the Genesee River. "Our sisters are sad at not seeing Dehgewanus," he said. "They miss her merry smile. They have spoken in praise of her virtue to our mother. Our mother waits to see her adopted daughter. Our whole family waits to welcome Dehgewanus."

After much thought, Sheninjee finally consented that Mary should visit her Seneca family and that she and their son could make the long journey with her three brothers. "You may go, Dehgewanus," Sheninjee said softly, "and I will join you there later. First I must go to the fort at the forks of the river and sell my furs. Then, when I have finished the winter's hunting, I will come to you."

Summer was already fading, and harvest time was at hand. The brothers agreed that the long journey to the Genesee country must be started at once in order to avoid the hazards of cold weather.

Mary lowered her eyes. "I shall miss you," she said to her tall, handsome Indian husband.

Sheninjee cupped Mary's chin firmly in the palm of his hand and raised her face until her blue eyes met his dark ones. "I shall miss you, too, Dehgewanus," he said. "I will join you and our son in the spring."

And so a race began against the onset of winter weather as Mary, with her three-month-old son strapped to her back in an Indian cradleboard, set out with her three Seneca brothers for the Seneca homeland in the Genesee Valley. It was to be an overland journey of almost seven hundred miles that the little group would make by canoe, on foot, and, at one point, on horseback. It was to be an incredibly arduous trek that would take them almost six months to complete.

Eleven

In the beginning of their journey, Little Billy and Young King and their other brother stopped frequently so that Mary could rest, knowing that she was not so accustomed as they were to walking all day. Sometimes, if they sensed that her legs were tiring, they invented excuses for stopping or for having *her* stop while one of them went off to scout the trail ahead. They did not, however, offer to carry the baby Thomas for her. That was woman's work.

After the first few days, Mary was able to keep pace without showing fatigue. The late summer days were warm and sunny, and the nights were mild. Most of the time they followed the path of a river, keeping to the high ground along its banks. They crossed wide prairie lands where they caught and roasted wild turkeys. At night they camped beside cool streams.

They came upon a deserted Indian town on a plateau overlooking the broad valley of the Sandusky River. The corn of the fields had been newly harvested, and there were signs that the town had been abandoned only recently, and in haste. After scouting the region, the brothers found foodstuffs and other possessions buried in well-concealed caches. Apparently the villagers intended to return. That would explain their leaving behind stores too bulky to carry in flight.

In the hidden cache were large provisions of beans, maple sugar, and honey, as well as the newly harvested corn, all carefully wrapped and concealed so that no moisture would spoil them. Mary and her brothers helped themselves to foodstuffs, taking what they could carry for their journey ahead.

As they prepared to leave, they discovered two horses and caught them. Pleased at the good fortune in replenishing their supplies and improving their means of travel, the little band turned eastward for the next and longest stage of their journey to the Genesee country.

Day after day they traversed relatively open and level land until they entered the forested Allegheny foothills. In a few places they followed a trail that showed signs of being well traveled. It led them up into deep-shaded mountains and then pointed them down and around the slopes into sunny valleys. Mary always felt a sense of relief when they emerged from the woods into the sunlight of the valleys. In most places the trail wound through endless stretches of dark and shadowy pines. The forest was silent and lonely and the trail was often indistinct. The sinister memory of another trek with Indians through dark mountain forests sent shivers up Mary's spine. This time, however, she was traveling as a trusted member of an Indian family, and she was carrying upon her back an Indian baby—hers and Sheninjee's. White folk would call the baby a half-breed, curling their lips to spit the word contemptuously. To Mary he was a beautiful baby with round blue eyes like hers and deep-toned skin and dark hair like his father's. She loved her son, and she hoped he would grow tall and strong to bear proudly his white grandfather's name.

How differently she thought of things now! How different her life might have been! Mary allowed her thoughts to drift idly. Would it have been a happier life? Easier, perhaps? She would never know. Many years later she remarked to her biographer that "one thing only marred my happiness . . . the recollection that I had once had tender parents, and a home that I loved."

The nights were turning colder now, and the party often camped on the mountain slopes. Mary gathered fallen leaves from the sycamores and maples to cover herself and the baby. Her thin blanket was not warm enough. And her summer clothing—all she had with her—offered little warmth.

The next inhabited place they came upon was the Indian town of Venango at the junction of French Creek and the Allegheny River, where Franklin, Pennsylvania, is today. Here stood a small fort garrisoned by English soldiers who had come across the mountains with General Forbes four years ago to seize the outpost from the French. The French had built the fort as a link in a chain of fortresses between Canada and Fort Duquesne to secure their hold on the Ohio lands. Now the Indians of the village played ball on the cleared ground outside the stockade walls, and Mary's Seneca brothers joined in the game.

Two days' journey north along the Allegheny from Venango brought the little party to Conowango Creek (now Warren, Pennsylvania). They had made good time, managing forty miles during each of the last two days, but Mary had found it uncomfortable riding astride the unsaddled horse behind one of her brothers. At Conowango Creek, however, their horses wandered away into the woods, and the brothers spent ten days pursuing them before they caught them. During their search they captured another stray horse, which would enable them to travel in greater comfort over the miles stretching ahead. Now only one horse would have to carry two riders. Despite the reward of an extra horse, the lost time was costly.

Heavy rains had begun to fall before they could be on their way again. The water came in cloudbursts, pelting the landscape and raising the level of the creek to a height that made crossing perilous. The brothers were hesitant even to attempt the crossing, but they ventured into the treacherous waters several times to test the depth and to observe the behavior of their horses. The horses whinnied with fright as they were prodded deeper into the swirling waters. When they lost their footing, they floundered—half swimming, half stumbling—back to solid ground.

The Indians debated whether to wait for the flood-waters to subside or to make another try. Little Billy wanted to wait; Young King insisted that they cross at once before the flood became worse. Their other brother, fearing that if they delayed now, they would be caught later in the heavy winter snowstorms, sided with Young King. And so they made ready for another try. Grimly Mary gave up half her blanket so that it could be torn into strips to blindfold the eyes of the horses. She used the remaining half to reinforce the strappings of the cradleboard on her back.

Sitting astride a spotted gray mare behind Young King and clinging tightly to his waist, Mary clutched her legs around the horse's belly with all her might. They had no saddle, only a deerhide rein and a bit made of bone. She was not really frightened, but she recognized the peril of their situation. She was not a good swimmer, and the stiff cradleboard strapped tight to her back would hamper her movements if she were thrown from the horse. Her greatest worry was the safety of her baby.

Young King leaned low over the mare's mane and

stroked her neck while he spoke soft Indian words of encouragement to her. Gently he nudged her forward into deeper waters. Bit by bit under his quiet persuasion, the mare inched ahead, feeling cautiously for each foothold. Ever so slowly they moved toward the opposite shore.

One of the other horses floundered and made the mare shy. She raised her head in protest, shaking loose the blindfold. The whites of her eyes showed in fear. Mary held tight and said nothing. Young King let the horse rest a brief moment before urging her forward again. Then the bottom dropped away. The mare whinnied and turned her head as if to start back, but her rider held fast to his lead. Instinctively the animal raised her hoofs and swam until she scraped bottom on the other side.

Once across the flooded creek they traveled over a path so crooked and overgrown that Mary wondered if they had lost their way. Little Billy, who had made the trip many times to and from the Ohio country, reassured her that they were not lost. Such trails, he explained, had been made long, long ago by wandering herds of buffalo. Usually the beasts had followed the highest ridges of ground paralleling a river. Later, Iroquois war parties traveled the same traces on single-file marches to make war on their Cherokee enemies to the south. Little Billy showed Mary blazes on tree trunks that recorded messages from one Indian warrior to another. Some blazes merely marked the trail. Others bore detailed messages. To Mary's untrained eyes, they appeared to be nothing more than notches on the tree trunk where bark had broken away.

With the drenching rains came the cold winds of winter. Each day the journey grew more difficult. Frost came early that year, destroying the unharvested crops of Indian farmers who dwelt along the way. The farmers had no grain to spare for travelers who passed over the trail, and Mary and her Seneca brothers often went hungry. Each day they traveled a shorter distance. Each day they rested more frequently and for longer periods of time before resuming their weary trek.

They grew weaker and weaker as the chilly days wore on. Mary feared for her baby. He had become listless and thin. Their meager diet had been reduced to what few edible roots they could dig in the forests. Even the horses grew weak from hunger. There was scant forage in the thick sunless woods for them to feed upon. Their ribs showed like skeletons'. At length the animals could support the travelers no more and had to be led, riderless.

By this time Mary's clothing was ripped and ragged beyond repair. It no longer protected her from the weather or from the scratches of the underbrush. Most of the time it lay clammy against her skin, wet clear through from the constant rains. How she longed for the warmth and protection of the snug home she had

shared with Sheninjee! When she and her brothers stopped to rest or to sleep now, they were all too weak from hunger to spare strength for making a shelter of boughs. It was all they could do to get a fire going. Nevertheless, the ragged travelers staggered on toward Little Beard's Town, making whatever distance they could each day.

Sharing the hardships and adventures of the trip had provided a kinship between Mary and her Indian brothers much deeper than that of her adoption into their family. The Senecas had come to know and respect the yellow-haired captive whom they had accepted as their sister. She had borne the discomforts and dangers of their journey with a fortitude they had never thought possible from a white woman—especially from one so fair and fragile. Not once had she shown bitterness at the hardships she was forced to endure. Not once had she asked them to spare her the burden of carrying the baby, Thomas. The brothers were proud to call her their sister.

"We are not far, little sister," Young King told her. "Do not be discouraged. We will make it to Genesee. We will trade our horses for food. It is more important to walk in health than to ride in sickness. Your son will be strong again."

Twelve

December's wintry winds swirled around Mary and her brothers as they struggled down the mountains into the valley of the Genesee River on the final leg of their journey. They were coming home. But for Mary it was a home she had never seen and there was a mother who was a total stranger.

Before them lay the crooked path of the Genesee, winding through stretches of wilderness, through forests of sugar maples, and alongside flatlands of shoulder-high grass. Only the nearness of their destination and the comforts awaiting them enabled the foot-weary travelers to continue their painful journey. They were weak with hunger, cold, and exhaustion.

After pausing briefly to rest at Caneadea, they pushed on through landscape so awesome that Mary, despite her exhaustion, gasped at its wild beauty. High above the narrow river, they threaded their way along a rocky precipice, hemmed to its edges by dense forests. Below them at the bottom of a deep gorge, the river cut a snakelike trough until its waters tumbled in white foam over three cataracts. Then, its wild power spent, it emerged lazily into the wide, plate-shaped Genesee Valley.

There was great rejoicing when the ragged little party reached Little Beard's Town. Mary was received lovingly by the family that had adopted her. The two sisters hugged her and fussed over the baby. Others of the town joined the family in celebrating with feasting and dancing the long-awaited arrival of the brothers and their white sister.

For the next several days, Mary's Seneca family took over caring for her and her baby. With wholesome food, plenty of rest, and the knowledge that she had someone to rely upon, Mary gradually lost her emaciated look, and her strength returned. Soon she was able to join the women in their daily chores and activities. Her baby began to fill out, too; his little brown body grew plump, and Mary cuddled him tightly to her. How he had grown! Sheninjee would not recognize him. She breathed a sigh of gratitude that Sheninjee had not seen his son at the end of the long journey when he had been so frail and sickly.

The life of Little Beard's Town delighted Mary. It was much larger than she had imagined it to be—it was the most important town of the Seneca Nation and its capital. Unlike the smaller villages that were moved whenever the Indians chose, an air of permanence hung over Little Beard's Town. Its buildings were sizable and laid out in sensible patterns. Countless acres for cornfields and gardens extended beyond the town and bespoke the diligence of generation after generation of Indian farmers. There were orchards of peach and pear and apple and wild plum trees.

There were many young women Mary's age. Most of them were anxious to be friendly with the white girl, although a few shied away from her. They treated her with a degree of awe and with great respect. Her knowledge of their language assured her participation in social affairs, and she found herself enjoying the busy pace of the Indian town. Never before had she lived among so many people. Her years with the Indians along the Ohio River had been spent in small encampments, and her life before that, on the farm on Marsh Creek, had been limited to her immediate family and occasionally a visit with neighbors.

At Little Beard's Town she lived in a longhouse that was shared by others of her Seneca family and also by other entire families. Often as many as fifteen families, usually relatives, shared the long rectangular bark dwellings. Each family unit had its own compartments on either side of a center aisle. The fire—one for every two families—burned on the yellow clay floor in the center aisle, its smoke curling up toward a hole in the roof. Bunklike cubicles lined each side of the long, narrow building and served as beds at night and benches during the day. From the rafters and cross-poles hung dried corn, pieces of dried pumpkin and squash strung together, snowshoes, baskets and tumplines, weapons and other paraphernalia owned by the occupants.

Before the last snows of winter had melted away, Mary joined the women of her family along with others of the town for the annual trip to the sugar camp some miles distant. Once each year in late March or early April, when the warm sunlit days alternated with chilly, frosty nights, the sap of the sugar maples began to flow. Then the Indian women, with the help of their children, would gather and prepare enough of the sweet sap to last them through the year.

First they cleaned and mended the containers of elm bark that were used to catch the sap as it flowed from a gash in the tree trunk. They had to make several new vessels to replace those too worn for repair. The bark containers were then hung from a peg of hardwood that had been wedged into the tree. Drop by drop the sweet watery sap filled the crude vessels, which Mary and the other young women and girls then carried to the fires. There the sap simmered in huge kettles until it became sirupy. When the sirup reached the correct consistency, it was poured into molds and allowed to harden.

The Indian women made a treat for the children by dropping scoopfuls of the boiling sirup onto a cold snowbank. It hardened immediately into a delicious candy, which melted delectably in the mouth. Roasted kernels of corn sweetened with the sirup were another treat relished by the youngsters. Children today call it caramel corn.

When they all returned home with their fresh supplies of sugar and sirup, the women of the town prepared for a festival at which all the Indians gave thanks to the stately maple trees for their sweet yield. Dancing and singing to the rhythmic beat of the water drums went on far into the night, along with feasting and sampling the new batch of maple sugar candies. The Indians called it the Sweetwater Festival.

With the coming of the spring rains, Mary began to watch hopefully for Sheninjee's arrival. Summer came on, and still he did not come. Her hope gave way to concern and finally to alarm. One day a runner arrived with a message for the young white woman. Sheninjee would not be coming, he said. He had taken sick at Wiishto not long after leaving Mary and their son, and there he had died.

Sheninjee dead? Mary did not want to believe it. For many weeks she grieved over the loss of her Indian husband. How would she raise her half-caste son? The Seneca family reminded her gently that she was their daughter and that the ties of the adoption ceremony bound her to them as closely as if she had been born to them. They would take care of her. They would help her teach her young son the things he must learn in order to grow into a fine, strong man. In word and in deed in the months ahead, they proved their promise.

Slowly a year passed. Mary's grief had at last begun to heal when a Dutchman, John Van Sice, who sometimes came to Little Beard's Town to trade, made known his intentions of returning Mary Jemison to the English authorities at Fort Niagara.

"I shall take you back to your own people," he told Mary.

"My people are dead," Mary answered.

"Yes, but you are a white woman," he said, stroking his beard. "You do not belong with the Indians." His voice became cajoling. "Come with me to Fort Niagara. You can make a new life for yourself. There is no need now for you to stay with these savages."

"They are good to me," Mary said. "They are the only friends I have."

"*I* am your friend," the Dutchman said. "I want to take you back to your own kind of people. Would I bother doing that if I were not your friend?"

"I must think about it," Mary said.

"Then hurry," he said rudely. "I have no time to wait for you to make up your mind. We will leave for Niagara tomorrow morning."

Ever since she had become a captive almost six years ago, Mary had thought of the day when she might return to a life among her own people. Now that the opportunity had come, she was confused by her reluctance to accept it. She was not sure that it was what she wanted. She needed time to think.

While she was pondering what her life might be like if she were to go back with the Dutch trader, she found out that Van Sice wanted to take her to the fort in order to collect bounty money paid by the English authorities for the return of white captives. Friend indeed! He gave neither hoot nor holler what happened to her after that. All he wanted was the money! She was no more important to him than a sack of grain or a copper kettle. Mary bristled at the thought of being sold as if she were a piece of merchandise.

She sought out the Dutchman. "Thank you just the same, Van Sice," she said, "but I prefer to stay where I am."

The greedy trader's eyes narrowed. "We shall see about that," he sneered. He said it as a threat, and Mary did not trust him. She avoided him for the rest of the day and was glad that he would be leaving town in the morning.

The next day Mary went alone to the garden at the edge of the cornfields. As always, she enjoyed working among the plants, and as she had learned from past experiences, hard work helped to relieve her troubled thoughts. She wondered now as she pulled weeds from among the bean plants if she had done the right thing in telling Van Sice that she preferred to stay with the Indians. Was it right to pass up the opportunity to go back because her pride had rebelled at the thought of being turned in for a bounty? Was false pride standing in the way of her going back among people of her own kind?

It was peaceful working in the quiet garden with only the rustling wind and the chirping crickets for company. The sun was warm upon her back. She rose from her bent-over position to stretch when, out of the corner of her eye, she saw the bearded man. He was crouching behind a row of bean plants that did not entirely hide him. So silent had been his approach that she had not heard a sound. As she stared in the direction of the bean patch, the Dutchman stood up. Mary saw the coil of rope that dangled from his belt, and at once she understood. He had come to get her, willingly or not, and she knew now that she could not go with him.

"Come, little white woman," he said. A wicked smile curled his lips. "It is time for us to start for Niagara."

Knowing that the trader would not listen to her, Mary ran from him into the cornfields. He ran after her, cursing under his breath. As fast as her legs would carry her, she crossed the cornfields in leaping strides and ran into the tall sweeping grass of the fields beyond. Although the grass grew taller than her head and afforded adequate cover, she could not be sure that her path through it could not be traced by her pursuer. So, she ran on and on, pacing herself after a while in order to conserve her strength. Long after the sun had passed its midday high, she reached a secluded green valley bounded by incredibly steep rock walls. She recognized the place. It was part of the beautiful area known as Gardeau that she had admired when she passed through it over a year and a half ago.

Fearing that the trader might be lying in wait somewhere, planning to catch her on her return to Little Beard's Town, Mary hid herself in a dirty abandoned hut, where she spent three lonely days and nights.

Thirteen

Mary worked her way back to the town slowly and cautiously, still half expecting the trader to leap at her from behind one of the trees or boulders alongside the trail. Her heart was heavy. Eventually she reached the safety of the longhouse.

The Seneca family had not dared to search for her, they said, for fear of leading the wily Dutchman to her. He had looked for her for two days, and he had kept watch on the members of the family. Finally, sullen and angry, he had left the village.

Soon thereafter, the chiefs of the town held a Council to discuss the attempted abduction of the white woman. "Is she not a legally adopted member of a Seneca family?" they reasoned with each other. Then, after lengthy consultation, they decreed that she should not be taken to the white authorities without her consent.

Scarcely a week had passed, however, before an elderly warrior of the tribe told Mary's brother Young King that he was not in agreement with the judgment of the Council, that Mary should be returned to the English authorities, and that it was his intention to take her to Niagara himself. Young King reminded the old warrior of the Council's decision. "Have you forgotten so quickly the judgment of the Council, old man?" he asked testily.

"The members of the Council speak foolishness," the old man said. "The small white woman is not a Seneca. Of what use is she to us? Why should I not turn her in? The English will pay. . . ." His voice trailed off as the younger man scowled menacingly at him.

"Greedy old man!" Young King raged. "You only want to turn her in for the money so you can buy rum. All you think of is firewater — the white man's firewater that makes you forget how old and useless you are!"

"Mind your tongue," the old warrior snapped. "I am old, but once I was a mighty warrior and a respected chief."

"The rum has sapped your vigor and diluted your judgment," Young King replied. "You shall not take the white woman. She is our sister. I will kill her before I will let you take her!"

"Ha!" the old man sneered. "Your bad temper will not help her. I shall take her. Wait and see." He turned his back and walked away.

Shaking with uncontrollable rage, Young King went to the longhouse and told one of his sisters of the old warrior's determination to take Mary to Niagara and of his own vow to kill Mary rather than see her taken against her will.

His sister was alarmed, for she did not doubt that he would carry out his threat if the old warrior forced him to. She found Mary. Grimly she told her of the plot.

"Your life is in great danger," she said. "Our brother threatens to kill you rather than see you taken against your will. The old one vows he will return you to the English. He says he does not agree with the judgment of the chiefs in Council. But Young King says the old man wants to turn you in only for the bounty so that he can buy firewater."

"What shall I do?" Mary asked, knowing before the question was answered that once again she must hide.

"Take young Thomas and hide in the high grasses beyond the town until the night is still," the sister directed. "When I bake corncakes this evening," she went on, "I will place one outside the door as a signal. If there is no cake, it will be safe for you to come in. If the cake is there, take it and run to the big spring on the south side of Samp's Creek. Hide there with your son until I send word to you. Go quickly! I fear for your life."

Mary carried young Thomas piggyback as she hurried away. The little boy would be three in a few months, and he was almost too heavy to carry, though still too young to move quickly by himself.

All day they hid among the sweeping grass. When

Thomas became restless, Mary plaited a make-believe scarecrow doll for him with reeds. She told him stories, keeping her voice to a whisper. She did everything and anything her weary brain could invent to keep him occupied so that he would stay quiet within the narrow confines of their hiding place. When the night had long fallen and the child slept soundly, Mary crept back to her sister's door to see what fate had declared for her.

Her hopes sagged when she saw the cake outside the door. Now she must flee again; hide again; fear for her life again. Must she always be running? Dejectedly she crept back to where little Thomas lay hidden. She sighed as she picked up his relaxed little sleeping body and began the long walk to Samp's Creek.

They reached the spring toward morning, and Mary sat down in exhaustion. She made a breakfast of the small corncake for herself and Thomas, washing it down with handfuls of water from the spring. Then she sank into a fitful sleep.

Alternately she slept and awakened. Might it be better, after all, if she went back to the white authorities? She *must* face her problem and make a decision once and for all. Twice now within a week's time she had been given a chance to be free, to be returned to her own people and to the civilization she had known as a child. And twice she had run away from the opportunity.

She forced her mind to pose questions: Were the whites her people, or were the Indians? If she were to go back to a life among the whites, where would she go and who would support her? How could she support herself and her little boy? What would it be like for her son to grow up as a half-breed among white people? What kind of life did she want for him?

Ma had said to her on the day they were parted, "Be strong." The loving memory jogged Mary's thoughts. Now was a time to be strong—to face the future with the courage and the dignity that Ma had tried to instill in her—the kind of courage Ma herself had shown.

Some of the answers came hard, but at length they came, and she resolved that she would face her future with the Indians, living as a Seneca of the Genesee country. Here her son would be raised as a member of a proud family who would love him and help him to grow into a dignified manhood. Here were her friends. And here was the family who had shown their love by treating her as one of them.

Having made her decision, Mary felt at peace. Even though she knew her fate still hung in the balance, depending upon the outcome of the quarrel between the elderly chief and her Seneca brother, she dropped into a serene sleep.

Toward noon Mary awoke with a start. Someone was coming. She grew numb with fear as she recognized the tall, lean form of Young King. Had he come to kill her? She trembled as he approached—still unable in the distance that separated them to make out the expression on his face.

At last he called out to her. "I have come to take you home. The old chief has gone to Niagara without you."

Tears of relief welled in Mary's eyes. Quickly she blinked them away. She took little Thomas by the hand and walked to meet her brother.

"We will go home," Young King said simply as he swung the little boy onto his shoulders. "It is peaceful there now."

With joy and with the certainty at last that her place was with the Indians, Mary Jemison began the journey home.

Epilogue

Mary Jemison lived the rest of her long and eventful life with the Indians of the Genesee country. In many ways it was the stormy life her father long ago had predicted in jest.

Mary eventually married a fierce Seneca warrior, Hogadowah. Six children were born to them—John, Jesse, Jane, Nancy, Betsey, and Polly—all named after Mary's relatives.

When the Revolutionary War broke out, Hogado-wah sided with the English and made war against the colonists, leaving Mary and the children at Little Beard's Town. Late in the war when colonial forces marched toward the Seneca capital to destroy it, Mary and her children fled with the other Indians. When they came back, they wept at the sight of what the soldiers had done. Everything was gone—their homes, their cattle, their food supplies, even their beautiful orchards. All had been burned to the ground and lay in blackened ruin. Rather than starve or freeze to death during the coming winter, the Senecas walked wearily back toward Buffalo.

But not Mary. Carrying two of her children on her back and beckoning the rest to follow, she headed for the secluded flatlands at Gardeau, where she had sought refuge once before. There, as she had hoped, the cornfields stood untouched and ready for harvest. Two runaway Negro slaves living in the same hut that had sheltered her over a decade ago were the only others there. They welcomed Mary's offer to help harvest the corn in exchange for a share of it and for shelter. In that way she and her children weathered one of the cruelest winters ever known to the Genesee Valley. In the spring she built a hut of her own there and planted corn and vegetables. Hogadowah stayed on the warpath long after the war had ended, harassing settlers in vengeful attacks.

Once again Mary was given the choice of returning to white civilization. The offer came from Young King, who had once threatened to kill her rather than let her be taken against her will. Mary's decision was not difficult this time, and even though her oldest son tried to persuade her to go to white friends, she stayed with the Senecas.

To show Mary how this pleased him, Young King made her a promise that some day she would have land of her own—land to live on without fear, land for her children to inherit. Before leaving the Genesee country for Canada, he spoke of his promise to his friend, Farmer's Brother, a Seneca chief. Soon afterward, Young King died.

Years later, in 1797, Farmer's Brother summoned Mary to the Great Council at Big Tree. There he won for her a claim of 18,000 acres of Genesee lands including her familiar Gardeau, finally fulfilling Young King's promise.

When white settlers moved into the valley, Mary rented land to some of them. She was helpful to those in need. She gave food from her own table to hungry families and seed to farmers who were too poor to buy it.

Then in a span of a few years, sorrow struck at her four times. In 1811 Hogadowah died and not long afterward, all three of Mary's sons, now grown to manhood, were tragically killed.

She began to sell pieces of her land to white families. In the spring of 1817, a special act of Congress declared Mary Jemison of the Senecas a citizen of the United States in order to confirm the title of her land so that she might sell it as she wished.

The settlers grew accustomed to the sight of the small, quick-stepping white woman in Indian garb. They called her "the White Woman of the Genesee," and they spoke of her with affection and great respect. Her advice often resolved misunderstandings between them and their Indian neighbors, and Mary's judgment at Council meetings was sought and received with attention. She occupied a unique position.

As a Seneca she was a respected member of the tribe, the owner of vast lands, and the wife of a great warrior. The white settlers recognized her as a spirited and brave woman who, though Indian by choice, was nevertheless one of them as well. Her wisdom and kindness seemed to blend the best qualities of each culture and earned her the trust and admiration of all her neighbors—Indian and white alike.

Toward the end of the year 1823, when Mary was eighty, she told her life's story to James Everett Seaver, who wrote it down and published it. Mary's own words best describe her way of life: "In regard to ourselves," she said, "just as we feel, we are."

Two years later the Senecas sold what remained of their Genesee lands and moved to reservations near Buffalo. Mary had disposed of all her land except for the two-acre plot she lived on with her daughters and their husbands and children. Her friends persuaded her to leave Gardeau in the summer of 1831 and move to the Buffalo Creek Reservation. There, at the age of ninety, she died on September 18, 1833.

Today Mary Jemison's grave is at Letchworth State Park beside the tumbling waters of the Genesee River in her beloved Gardeau. It is marked by a statue showing her as she arrived in the Genesee country carrying her first-born son on her back.

A short time before she died, Mary told a missionary seeking to convert her to Christianity that she did not know how to pray. Although the White Woman of the Genesee had forgotten the words of the Christian prayers she learned in her childhood, she had lived their meanings in truth and in kindness throughout all her life.

Notes

More than twenty years after her capture, Mary Jemison learned that her two older brothers, John and Thomas, Jr., had escaped from behind the barn when the war party raided the Jemison farm and eventually made their way to relatives in Virginia.

Mary learned also that she and her family were followed by a rescue party as far as the edge of the swamp. There the rescuers found the remains of the Jemison family and of Mrs. Mann and her children. Because there was no trace of a trail beyond that spot, they abandoned further pursuit, assuming there were no survivors.

In most accounts of Mary Jemison's story, her Seneca husband, Hogadowah, is called Hiokatoo, and one of the Indian brothers of her adopted family is called Kaujisestaugeau. I am grateful to Dr. Charles E. Bartlett of Castile, New York, for sharing his research that corrects these names and identifies Mary's Seneca brothers as Gayengontwen (Young King) and Jiska-akak (Little Billy).

Dr. Bartlett, a dentist and a scholar of the Senecas, explains that when Mary Jemison told her life's story to James Everett Seaver, she was over eighty and toothless, except for a few front lower teeth. Her Seneca pronunciations were hard to understand, and the erroneous spellings published by Seaver persisted, in the absence of written Seneca records, to the present day. The story of Dr. Bartlett's findings are recorded in Volume XIX, No. 3 (April, 1966) of *Historical Wyoming*.

Bibliography

Carmer, Carl, *Dark Trees to the Wind*, New York, William Sloane Associates, 1949.

Carmer, Carl, *Listen for a Lonesome Drum*, New York, William Sloane Associates, 1936.

Clune, Henry, *The Genesee*, New York, Holt, Rinehart & Winston, 1964.

Cornplanter, Jesse, *Legends of the Longhouse*, Philadelphia and New York, J. B. Lippincott Company, 1938.

Hamilton, Edward P., *The French and Indian Wars*, New York, Doubleday, 1962.

Federal Writers Project, *Guide Books to Pennsylvania, New York,* and *Ohio,* New York, Oxford University Press, 1940.

LaFarge, Oliver, *A Pictorial History of the American Indian*, New York, Crown Publishers, Inc., 1956.

Lossing, Benson, J., *Pictorial Fieldbook of the Revolution*, 2 vols., New York, Harper & Brothers, 1855.

Parkman, Francis, *A Half-Century of Conflict* ("France and England in North America"), Boston, Little, Brown & Company, 1929.

Parkman, Francis, *Conspiracy of Pontiac,* Boston, Little, Brown and Company, 1929.

Seaver, James Everett, *A Narrative of the Life of Mary Jemison,* Canandaigua, New York, 1824 (as reproduced in the 22nd edition published by The American Scenic & Historic Preservation Society, New York, 1925).

Van Every, Dale, *Forth to the Wilderness* ("The First American Frontier, 1754–1774"), New York, New American Library, 1961.

Wallace, Paul A. W., *Indians in Pennsylvania,* Harrisburg, Pennsylvania, The Pennsylvania Historical & Museum Commission, 1961.